E-Governance

E-Governance

A Change Management Tool

P. Panneervel

RAWAT PUBLICATIONS
Jaipur and New Delhi

ISBN 81-7033-919-7 (hardback)
ISBN 81-7033-920-0 (paperback)

Distributed by
Gurjar Grantharatna Karyalaya
Opp. Ratanpole Naka, Gandhi Road, Ahmedabad - 380 001
Phone: 079 22149660 Fax: 079 22144663
E-mail: goorjar@yahoo.com Website: www.gurjar.biz

Published by
Prem Rawat for *Rawat Publications*
Satyam Apts., Sector 3, Jawahar Nagar, Jaipur 302 004 (India)
Phone: 0141 265 1748 / 7006 Fax: 0141 265 1748
E-mail: info@rawatbooks.com
Website: www.rawatbooks.com

Delhi Office
4858/24, Ansari Road, Daryaganj, New Delhi 110 002
Phone: 011-23263290

Typeset by Rawat Computers, Jaipur
Printed at Chaman Enterprises, New Delhi

Contents

Foreword 7
Preface 9
Acknowledgements 13
Acronyms 15
List of Tables 17
List of Figures 19

1 E-Governance Concepts 21
2 Smart Card-Based Driving Licence 35
3 Automation of Inter-State Border Transport Check-Posts 63
4 Optical Card Registration Certificate Book 95
5 Integrated Transport Management Information System 113
6 Urban E-Governance 131
7 E-Learning in Ahmedabad Schools 161
8 Change Management 175
9 Lessons 193

Annexures 215
Bibliography 233
Glossary 235
Index 247

Foreword

Improvement in the delivery of government services is an important issue for countries like India, as the cost of inefficiency is largely borne by the poor. India is home to a large number of pioneers of electronic service delivery systems in different sectors. According to anecdotal evidence, many of these projects have delivered significant benefits to citizens. One of the key challenges is to scale-up the successful pilot projects to nationwide projects. The Central Government has already developed an ambitious e-governance programme and is likely to make significant investments in automated transaction systems and service delivery applications in a variety of departments.

It is my privilege to write the foreword for this book, which is authored by Mr. Panneervel. Mr. Panneervel is a pioneer in using ICT in the state of Gujarat and has a rich experience of implementing innovative ICT applications. This book, which represents some of the useful applications built by the author himself, will help in furthering the progress of e-governance by providing an inner view of benefits from it. Certain critical factors contributing to success have also been discussed, which can act as guidelines for new projects.

One key feature of these applications is the experimentation with new technologies. Gujarat was the first state to introduce smart card-based driving licence for its citizens. Subsequently, in

Gujarat, check-post application video cameras were installed to capture images of number plates of any truck and then convert them to retrieve data about the tax and load carrying capacity of the truck from a database. Video cameras were, in fact, placed to serve as intelligent eyes to transact and monitor the check-post activities, which were then connected to headquarters, located in Ahmedabad.

There is much to learn from these cases that illustrate the advantages as well as challenges to be faced when adopting a new technology in an existing system. Most of these projects were completed in a short time-frame of one year. A lot of project management, system approach and skilful change management were required to successfully implement the projects. The most significant challenge in implementing ICT applications in India is to overcome the resistance from government employees, who are directly affected. ICT applications can reduce the discretionary power of a civil servant and make decision-making processes and information more transparent. This results in a loss of power and authority to favour some citizens at the expense of others. The author has interestingly described the processes that were used to manage change and has also drawn lessons from different contexts in which the applications were designed and built like transport, urban governance and education.

There are many books on e-governance but most of them talk about the technology and not about the change management processes which play a key role in implementing the projects. This book fills up the gap in the pool of knowledge that needs to be built to help guide practitioners. I hope, the book will not only inspire others to take up the challenges of e-governance applications but also lead us towards more efficient management.

Subhash Bhatnagar
Indian Institute of Management, Ahmedabad

Preface

Developments in the Information and Communication Technology (ICT) fields have been taking place at a rapid pace. India with its e-literate resources is fast emerging as a major initiator in e-governance adoption. This is despite the challenges arising out of conditions related to awareness, literacy, basic infrastructure, bandwidth issues and multilingual and cultural issues. Added to this is the issue of enabling members of the public service make the transition from the traditional approaches to a new and evolving environment that is defined by ICT development. To keep pace with the surrounding development, governments will need mechanisms to respond to these changes. The disciplines of knowledge management and change management provide important tools for public administrators.

This book is about governance and how it can be changed with application of 'e'. It is about the transformation which 'e'-application can bring about in public administration, how we can use modern information and communication technologies, organizational principles, and knowledge to create a citizen-centric good governance system.

Primarily, the book illustrates six e-governance projects undertaken by the author during the course of his postings as Commissioner of Transport, Government of Gujarat; Municipal Commissioner, Ahmedabad Municipal Corporation, Ahmedabad;

and Principal Secretary (Education), Government of Gujarat. The technological pattern and the variation from one project to the other project are wide. It leaves to the readers to perceive for themselves about the methods adopted to implement these e-governance projects. The methodology adopted to bring in change management process to implement e-governance project is different from one project to other. These experiments and the experiences throw light on how various stakeholders participated in transforming paper-based system to a new e-based governance system.

The role of a large number of employees and the users involved in designing the solution and implementing the same successfully cannot be undermined. The relevance of these cases may not be applicable to a variety of functions of the government, but the process involved in motivating the employees to make a commitment to bring in change in their work environment may be unique and perhaps would set the ball rolling to replicate similar projects in e-governance.

When a host of consultants and IT companies seek business in providing solutions to various government activities, the case studies presented in involving employees to come out with in-house solutions is a benchmark. In a hierarchical and deceptively feudal-based management structure, 'jumping levels' with open expression of solutions are unacceptable and may warrant disciplinary actions against the employees. Work environment of such nature may neither provide creative atmosphere nor allow employees to pool intricate organizational information and solutions. Hence, a mere thought of evolving in-house e-governance solution in any state government organization is a high-risk project. It involves high percentage of internal marketing processes to change the attitudes of the employees, which is presented in this book through projects of varied nature that were implemented in the Gujarat state.

The book is intended to serve a wide audience, especially those working in public administration, universities and educational institutions, non-governmental organizations and professionals. The case studies illustrated narrate experience in such a way that it gives indication to the possibility of the problems likely to be faced in future implementation by practitioners, project managers, government officers, non-government agencies etc. A specific focus is also given to the emerging e-governance experts from the students community.

The book contains nine chapters. Chapter 1, which is introductory chapter of the book, provides a starting point for the subject matter and themes to be discussed in this book. It also attempts to clarify some of the basic concepts of e-governance. This is done first by distinguishing government and governance, then defining e-governance and lastly identifying and discussing the process of transformations in governance, namely, change management process.

Chapter 2 provides an analytical description of development and implementation process of smart card-based driving licence system in Gujarat. The smart card-based driving licence with biometric identification, introduced by Government of Gujarat in the year 1999, was the first of its kind in the world. Since then, this is the largest smart card project operating in the world. The challenges faced during the process of implementation have also been dealt with. The costs and benefits of the digital system have also been addressed adequately.

Chapter 3 deals with the e-governance application to the motor vehicle tax collection system in transport sector. As expected, like all major revenue contributing sectors, the transport sector too had been burdened with all the inefficiencies and was accompanied by the culture of corruption. The state implemented e-governance application in the form of a fully automated inter-state border checks posts in 1999 and the same has been presented in this chapter. The chapter also discusses how the implementation of the project reduced corrupt practices and enabled the state to increase its revenue from the source by multiple times.

Introduction of Optical Card RC Book as a logical extension of the e-governance initiatives carried out by the Transport

Department has been dealt with in Chapter 4. A smart card device, similar to that of the driving licence but with provision for holding large amount of information, has been designed.

In Chapter 5, Integrated Management Information System in the Transport Department has been described. The matter of this chapter is this final application of the Transport Department.

The Ahmedabad Municipal Corporation performs several civic duties and collects various taxes and charges. The system required being more transparent, accountable, and bringing in citizen focus. The process of transforming governance to become citizen-centric through e-governance application has been the focus of Chapter 6.

Use of information technology in municipal schools, located in Ahmedabad Municipal Corporation jurisdiction, was attempted through School-Net Project. Chapter 7 describes the project, how the teachers and the scholars developed course contents using computer-aided tools.

Chapter 8 explains how the process of change management was achieved through e-application.

Chapter 9, the last chapter of the book, provides an approach towards developing e-governance applications. Lessons in the form of critical success factors have also been highlighted as lessons learnt.

Acknowledgements

Getting to implement various projects has been a difficult but satisfying process. Putting together this book has also been a long process. In undertaking these, I received help and encouragement from many sources.

The Government of Gujarat has permitted me to share the experiences and lessons learnt through implementation of the projects to larger audience. I express my gratitude towards the government for the same.

I thank all my colleagues of the State Government and Ahmedabad Municipal Corporation for their whole-hearted participation in developing and implementing the projects.

Encouragement and support received from my colleagues in the service, academicians and professionals from the field saw me through the implementation of these innovative and a kind of first in the world e-governance projects. I am indebted to all and owe my sincere thanks.

The consultants the backbone of the projects who accepted innovative ideas and successfully converted them into reality deserves highest laurels.

My gratitude goes to Prof. Bhatnagar of Indian Institute of Management for his valuable comments on the draft manuscript and also for writing foreword to the book. But, for the motivation and encouragement from Prof. H.M. Shivanand Swamy and Ms. Neha Panchal of CEPT, Ahmedabad, this book would not have come out in this form. My sincere thanks to them.

Special thanks goes to the publishing team at Rawat Publications.

My special thanks goes to my wife—Deepika and to my children—Shivani and Sarvanan for always being there to provide the much needed encouragement and support that saw me through the successful implementation of the projects as well as completion of this book.

P. Panneervel

Acronyms

AMC	Ahmedabad Municipal Corporation
ARTO	Assistant Regional Transport Officer
CP	Check-Post
CoT	Commissioner of Transport
DBMS	Database Management System
DoT	Department of Telecommunication
e-GIF	E-governance Interoperability Framework
GIS	Geographical Information System
GP	Gate Pass
HO	Head Office
ICT	Information and Communication Technology
IIM	Indian Institute of Management
IIT	Indian Institute of Technology
INDEXT-B	Industrial Development Extension Bureau
LAN	Local Area Network
LPR	Licence Plate Recognition
MIS	Management Information System

MT	Metric Tonne
NBCC	National Building Construction Corporation
NIC	Network Interface Card
NID	National Institute of Design
NP	National Permit
PC	Personal Computer
PIN	Personal Identification Number
RC	Registered Certificate
RDBMS	Relational Database Management System
RTO	Regional Transport Office
TSP	Total Solution Provider
UNDP	United Nations Development Programme
UPS	Uninterrupted Power Supply
WAN	Wide Area Network

List of Tables

1.1 Government vs governance 23
1.2 E-government vs e-governance 26

2.1 Road accidents in Gujarat 38
2.2 Comparisons between paper and smart licences 59

3.1 Income of check-posts from 1997-98 to 2004-05 93

4.1 Growth of vehicle population 97
4.2 Rates charged in different states for vehicle registration certificate 106
4.3 Smart optical card-based vehicle registration certificate issued in Gujarat 108
4.4 Increased tax income 109

5.1 Application modules 120
5.2 Growth in vehicle population 121
5.3 Increase in income 127

6.1 Ahmedabad: Area and population growth 132
6.2 Property tax collection through city civic centres 151
6.3 Property tax transactions and collections through banks and webs 152
6.4 Category-wise complaints summary 153

6.5 Transactions made through city civic centres 155

7.1 Lessons created from standard 1 to 7 169

8.1 Social transition 189

List of Figures

1.1	Interactions between stakeholders in e-governance	27
2.1	Persons affected by road accidents in Gujarat	37
2.2	Paper driving licence	39
2.3	Biometric Technology Today declaring Gujarat as the first authority in the world to use biometric identification	48
2.4	Data capture and personalization of the system	51
2.5	Issuing of smart card-based driving licence	52
2.6	Paper licence to smart card licence	53
2.7	Smart driving licence system	56
3.1	Location of inter-state check-posts	70
3.2	Key components of the automated check-post	77
3.3	Functioning of the check-posts	79
3.4	Computerised licence plate recognition system	83
3.5	Central monitoring office	85
3.6	Check-post clearance procedure	86
3.7	Times of India, September 6, 2000	90
3.8	Increased revenues of check-posts	92
4.1	Putting it altogether in an optical card	100
4.2	Smart optical RC book	101
4.3	RC database record	103

4.4	Writing on chips	104
4.5	Biometrics recording	104
4.6	Writing on optical strip (storage data)	104
4.7	Times of India, September 7, 2000	107
4.8	Increased tax revenue	108
4.9	System architecture	110
5.1	Tax assessment and collection from new motor vehicles	116
5.2	Tax assessment and collection from registered commercial vehicles	117
5.3	Accounts and audit trial	118
5.4	Application system overview	122
5.5	WAN connections from field offices and check-posts	123
5.6	System network	124
5.7	Increase in income	130
6.1	Organizational structure of the administrative wing of AMC	135
6.2	Stakeholders vicious circle	138
6.3	Objectives of the reform process	140
6.4	Solutions	141
6.5	AMC e-governance system architecture	144
6.6	City civic centres	145
6.7	Location of six city civic centres	146
6.8	e-governance applications	148
6.9	Resource utilization	148
6.10	Revenue from property tax	150
6.11	Public convenience	154
7.1	Distribution of course content	166
7.2	Zonal laboratories for course content development	167
7.3	Teachers training and implementation in progress	171
7.4	Teaching in progress	171
7.5	A lesson prepared by a student	171
8.1	Role of change management in the process	180
9.1	Three-dimensional configure model for e-governance	203

1

E-Governance Concepts

Developments in the information and communication technology (ICT) have been taking place at a rapid pace. India with its e-literate resources is fast emerging as a major initiator in e-governance adoption. This is despite the challenges arising out of conditions related to awareness, literacy, basic infrastructure, bandwidth issues and multilingual and cultural issues. Added to this is the issue of enabling members of the public service make the transition from the traditional approaches to a new and evolving environment that is defined by ICT development. To keep pace with the surrounding development, governments will need mechanisms to respond to these changes. The disciplines of knowledge management and change management provide important tools for public administrators.

With 'e' gaining significance, other core aspects are often neglected. It is necessary to always remember that 'e' is only a prefix. Similarly, the terms 'government' and 'governance' are also used interchangeably. Though they are related, they are not the same. Further, the process of e-governance is just not about digitalizing government information. It is bringing about change in the stakeholders in their processes. This is the theme of this book. This chapter attempts to clarify some of the basic concepts of e-governance.

Government vs governance

The terms 'government' and 'governance' are currently in widespread use, sometimes interchangeably. It is important to develop a distinction between the two. Professor Donald F. Kettl's[1] recent book, *The Transformation of Governance* on the historical analysis of American public administration provides some good discussion on government vs governance:

— Government is an institutional superstructure that society uses to translate politics into policies and legislations.

— Governance is the outcome of the interaction of government, the public service and citizens throughout the political process, policy development, programme design and service delivery.

— Governments are specialized institutions that contribute to governance. Representative governments seek and receive citizen support, but they also need the active cooperation of their public servants.

— Governance is the outcome of politics, policies and programmes.

The institution of government involves a narrower range of considerations than the wider functions of governance. The function of governance involves a broader range of considerations than the structures of government. Good municipal governance depends on the representative quality and efficiency of local government.

If we look at the above-mentioned characteristics of government, they together convey the concept of dominance, orderliness and permanence. This also means that governments by nature are conservative organizations and slow to adapt to change.

---

1. As quoted by Riley Thomas B. in International Tracking Survey Report '03, No. 04 (2003), E-government vs E-governance: Examining the differences in a changing public sector climate.

Table 1.1
Government vs governance

Government	*Governance*
Superstructure	Functionality
Decisions	Processes
Rules	Goals
Roles	Performance
Implementation	Coordination
Outputs	Outcomes

Source: Riley Thomas B. (May, 2003), E-government vs E-governance: Examining the differences in a changing public sector climate.

Governance is the link between government and its broader environment—political, administration and social—and therefore it is more to deal with the functionality or activities related to it. Governance is also distinct from government in a way that it concerns long-term processes rather than immediate decisions.

UNDP defines governance as the exercise of economic, political and administrative authority to manage a country's affairs. It is understood that for good governance public support is a must and good governance has to be, among other things, participatory, transparent and accountable to people.

Governance is the art of public leadership. There are three distinct dimensions of governance:[2]

- The form of political regime;
- The process by which authority is exercised in the management of a country's economic and social resources; and
- The capacity of governments to design, formulate and implement policies and discharge functions.

The criteria that constitute good governance have been drawn from these three dimensions, and include:

2. Novartis Foundation for Sustainable Development as quoted in http://www.gdrc.org/u-gov/governance-define.html.

- Legitimacy of government (degree of 'democratization');
- Accountability of political and official elements of government (media freedom, transparency of decision-making, accountability mechanisms);
- Competence of governments to formulate policies and deliver services; and
- Respect for human rights and rule of law (individual and group rights and security, framework for economic and social activity, participation).

Governance refers to the relationship between civil society and the state, between those who rule and those who are ruled, and the government and the governed.[3] It is also understood as referring to the manner in which power is exercised in the management of economic and social resources for development.

Better governance is a more difficult task in comparison to better government because, in addition to internal management issues, governance also deals with matters related to public or customers.

Application of ICT in government sector

With increasing awareness about information and communication technology (ICT), information systems continue to proliferate all over the world at a breathtaking pace. ICT has made a profound impact on our lives and times. The emergence of web-based delivery system has increased the relevance of these tools in the collection, collation and sharing of information at low cost. Above all, this technology holds out the promise of transforming societies in the developing world. For instance, it can help social sectors like education, health, rural development and other areas to reach out and deliver the goods and services to distant consumers. Hence, it is important to maximize the use of ICT tools and applications for successful transformation of government delivery systems with minimized cost and maximized speed.

New information and communication technologies can also make significant contributions towards achievements of good

3. Mc Carney, Halfani and Rodriguez, 1998.

governance goals. But, government programmes have a number of characteristics that make their information needs different from those of the other corporate and business organizations. These include:

- A demand-driven approach, often with limited management capacity.
- A large number of programme implementing agencies, often with limited management capacity.
- A very large number of beneficiaries, with disbursements and delivery taking place daily.
- A variety of procurement methods, with a preponderance of community-based procurement.
- Operations in different departments require wide range of skills, motivating approaches, service providers and contractors.
- Frequent decentralization and centralization of management activities.
- Frequent contracting of important infrastructure activities.
- An anti-poverty agenda requiring the selection and monitoring of specific indicators for evaluating impact.
- Multiple stakeholders (citizens, communities, government, political executives, bureaucracy, employees, contractors, non-governmental organizations etc.), each with distinct information needs.
- Political visibility making transparency and efficiency all the more important.

Therefore, the strategies and implementation task of using ICT in government sector demands advanced vision, skills at higher authority level and cooperation from all.

What is e-governance?

Imagine a situation where interaction with the government can be done through one counter, 24 hours a day, seven days a week, without waiting in queues at government offices! This is possible if governments are willing to use electronic means such as Internet. Each citizen can make contact with the government through a website where all forms, laws, news and other information will be available. Many definitions exist for e-governance. Before defining e-governance, it is important to understand the difference between e-government and e-governance (Table 1.2).

Table 1.2
E-government vs e-governance

E-government	*E-governance*
Electronic service delivery	Electronic consultation
Electronic workflow	Electronic controllership
Electronic voting	Electronic engagement
Electronic productivity	Networked societal guidance

Source: As in Table 1.1.

E-government is the application of ICT to improve the efficiency and accountability of government, whereas, e-governance depends on the use of ICT by mobilizing government resources, and utilizing the internal information resources by the government employees with the help of citizens' acceptability to the changes taking place to provide better services to them.

E-governance can also be defined as the application of electronic means in the:

— interaction between government and citizens and government and businesses, and

— internal government operations to simplify and improve democratic, government and business aspects of the governance.

In developing countries, governments are beginning to use e-government applications to improve their interactions with citizens and businesses and also automate their internal operations (Figure 1.1). Common applications of e-government include online delivery of government information and services, e-procurement, web-based licensing and registration, online

Figure 1.1

Interactions between stakeholders in e-governance

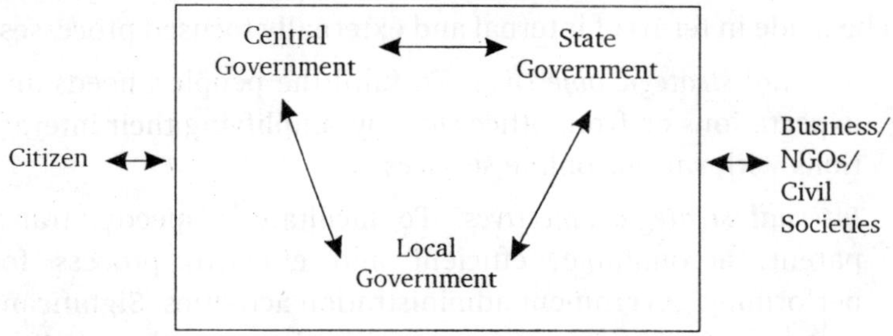

taxation and intra-governmental systems etc. The development related to Geographical Information Systems (GIS) has expanded the scope further.

The success of e-governance depends on the use of ICT in mobilization of government resources and utilization of these scarce resources with an aim to provide better services to citizens. The secret lies in doing away with discretionary powers vested in the hands of a few officials and provide easy access to all relevant information.

Objectives of e-governance

E-governance is a current reality for developing countries and the main objectives of an e-governance should be:

- to provide citizens access to information and knowledge about the political process, services and choices available;
- to make possible the transition from passive information access to active citizens' participation by
  - — informing the citizens,
  - — representing the citizens,
  - — encouraging the citizens to vote,
  - — consulting the citizens, and
  - — involving the citizens; and
- to make the system more efficient, more effective, and improve government process.

E-governance is much more than just a government website on Internet. The distinctions between the e-governance objectives can be made in terms of internal and externally focused processes:

- *External strategic objectives:* To fulfil the people's needs and expectations on front office side, by simplifying their interactions with various online services.
- *Internal strategic objectives:* To facilitate a speedy, transparent, accountable, efficient and effective process for performing government administration activities. Significant cost savings in government operations can be the result of this.

Challenges for e-governance

Uniformly, all government agencies accept that transparent, speedy and quality delivery systems can be built by leveraging ICT. Difference in perception exists on implementation processes. Most state governments feel that outsourcing would be the best method. But, the efforts put in during last one decade show that there is a great need to involve all stakeholders. Most often, the systems are designed giving more focus to technology than the intricate internal processes taking place within the department. Transforming these manual processes to system processes needs high-level involvement of government employees right from the initial stage itself. These information processes need to be converted to gradual translation of new applications. Here, the government employees' involvement starts from system design to implementation and operation.

These change reform processes also warrant training to the citizens. Change in voluntary behaviour by all the stakeholders needs high-level in-house activities than outsourcing. While it is true that high-level stakeholders' participation is essential, it is equally important to outsource ICT to implement, operate and maintain the systems. Balancing in-house activities and outsourcing technologies need integration right from the beginning as well as from top to bottom. The challenges are many, which can be broadly categorized as tactical and strategic.

Tactical challenges

In order to avoid failures and achieve success, it is important to motivate all the stakeholders and balance the change management process. The whole process has to be tailor-made so that it suits the local conditions for easier implementation. Certain issues have to be considered to decrease the gap between the design and actual implementation of the system. These are:

- Instead of reinventing the wheel, examine what has been done in developed countries for similar needs.
- Sufficient time should be given for needs assessment (feasibility study) what IT capacities to be used for what activity.
- There should be a common central database and all information needs of having same module should be integrated into a single flexible system.
- Within project modularity, certain level of flexibility should be possible.
- Base work with all required information should be ready at the time of project implementation.
- There should not be a lack of continuity from design to implementation to avoid delays.
- Regular evaluation (once a year) of the project is must in order to pick-up problems early.

Strategic challenges

No two governments can work the same way even though they perform largely the same tasks and share common problems. Each has its own culture, its own decision-making process, its own time frames, goals and objectives. Nevertheless, governments today have to operate at many levels from local to global and to do that successfully they must cooperate rather than confront each other. Internet technology can also help governments at different levels to get over potential antagonism by giving them an effective means to communicate, share data and provide integrated services across geographical, jurisdictional and programme boundaries.

As soon as the standards and policies are agreed upon with technical infrastructure in place, connections are set to enable data sharing with other jurisdictions and Internet applications are developed. Services are ready to roll out on a new government-wise portal and then a government employee, who is suddenly expected to work with someone from another agency, may find it difficult to accept the new working environment.

Factorial resistance is the greatest obstacle to the integrated online public services. There will be employees who resent to intrusion of technology in their daily routine and kneeling to hold familiar ways, no matter how well process improves. There are also employees, who have a natural tendency to hoard information, leak them and discredit data that others have developed. Inadequate and incomplete knowledge and data transfer, not only endangers the integrity of the work but also makes it cumbersome to carry forward. This requires a mindset change and is essential if bureaucrats are to work for wider government objectives rather than narrower departmental ones. Staff at both the government and personal levels need to be convinced that cyber space is more a space to work in the same old way and that "the way we have always done it" is no longer always the best way to do it.

There will be certain changes in the working system after e-governance for which strategies have to be thought in advance:

- Government communication and transactions with citizens and enterprises over the Internet: one-stop government, single-window service, seamless government.
- Frameworks and guidelines for e-government and e-governance.
- Institutional change and IT-driven modernization of public governance structures.
- Transnational e-government projects and standards.

- International and regional projects, case studies and international comparisons.
- Strategies, implementation policies and best practices.
- Redesigning cooperation within and between agencies.
- Sustaining business processes, collaborative activities, legal interpretation and administrative decision-making in a virtual space.
- E-democracy strategies, citizens' participation in local public affairs.
- Legal and organizational provisions, technical instruments, citizen cards, digital signatures.
- Standards for information interchange and processes, interoperability and semantic standardization.
- New organizational arrangements: ad-hoc cooperation and coalition between public agencies and public-private partnerships.
- Legal frameworks for e-government and e-governance.
- Political and societal implications of e-government and e-governance.

Change management

The biggest challenge in implementing e-governance solution is not the technology, but the employees and the awareness of the users. The process to involve the employees right from the design stage to operational stage may be lengthy and cumbersome but essential.

What is managing change?

Change management is the plan and implementation of programmes designed to bring about managerial and process change, using concepts from commercial marketing.[4] The goal of change management is to change behaviour, particularly problem

4. Centre of Change Management, University of Strathclyde, UK website.

behaviour.[5] It is basically application of concepts and tools from the commercial world to influence the voluntary behaviour of stakeholders to improve their lives and the society. In case of change in public regime like government department, requirements for either continuity or change can be mandated from above, but only implemented from below. Change management, therefore, becomes as much a question of personnel management as of programme management.

Hence, accomplishing governmental change management in this new environment will involve not only delegation from top executives to local branches and teams, but also within such local units from supervisors and team leaders to the members implementing the change. A situation is created in which everyone takes ownership of the change process and its consequences and when it is actually implemented, organizational units face some real challenges.

Various aspects of change are often resisted because those involved in are of "two minds" regarding the desirability of the new arrangement. Changes have both advantages and disadvantages, benefits and costs. People may feel that the advantages and benefits are desirable but are outweighed by expected disadvantages and costs. This is quite typical, and if the prospective change is not to be sabotaged, the people involved must resolve their conflicts of value regarding the change. These conflicts of value can only be effectively resolved through a series of group workshops in which the conflicts of value and their organizational implications are:

- publicly acknowledged;
- listed and grouped;
- confronted and discussed; and
- aligned in support of the organizational objectives.

---

5. Andreasen, A.R. (1995), *Marketing Social Change: Changing Behaviour to Promote Health, Social Development, and the Environment*. San Francisco: Jossey-Bass Publications.

In other words, before going for change in the existing system, all the stakeholders have to be clear about *what, why and how* are they planning for the change management. People have to believe that the change is worthwhile, feasible, authorized and adequately resourced. Only when these aspects are aligned and the people involved are committed to them, does there exist the social conditions for change within the group. In this case, change management is all about how members of the public service make the transition from the traditional approaches to the new era of management through ICT.

Why manage change?

It is a common impression that development in government processes and reforms is happening in breathtaking pace in developed countries whereas in developing countries lengthy procedures and red tapes lead public delivery systems to chaos. The reason can be due to developed countries leverage technologies to the optimal level to bring in change management re-engineering processes in all its functions and deliveries to the citizen. Leveraging e-governance as a tool brings in citizen-centric change management processes. The involvement of government policies, government employees, technological innovations, citizens' participation and re-engineering processes is inevitable to bring in positive reform measures. The concepts of commercial marketing techniques like social marketing or internal marketing techniques can also be applied to motivate the voluntary behaviour of the stakeholders. Because of the change in delivery processes, the results are visible and transparent, and this can be termed as change management.

The stakeholders' involvement is very high in e-governance processes and, therefore, change management concept needs to be applied extensively to bring in sustainable system improvement in delivery systems by leveraging ICT. Change should be worthwhile and then well managed.

E-governance: A tool to achieve change management

The progress of a country depends in no small measure on the quality of its governance. While a democratic government may lay the foundation for good governance, a vigilant and active citizenry is essential to its sustenance. Nowhere is this need more evident than in the management of public sector services for which citizens depend largely on their government. The quality of governance is enhanced when government as a whole and public agencies in particular become open to new ideas and responsive to citizens. Responsiveness in turn is improved when citizens are well informed and collectively seek better performance from these agencies.

2

Smart Card-Based Driving Licence

Smart card-based driving licence with biometric identification, introduced by Government of Gujarat in the year 1999, was the first of its kind in the world. Since then, this is the largest smart card project operating in the world. It has a memory chip of 1 kb that is mapped to four parts partly to store permanent information and partly to maintain and operate dynamic information. As of now, about five million smart card driving licences have been issued in the state of Gujarat. After the 9/11 tragedy, the United States of America also studied the smart card system for replication. Later they brought a parliamentary bill to introduce the Gujarat model of biometric based smart card driving licence system in February 2002. Dr. Don Davis, Smart Card Advisor to US, was in constant touch with the author (then Transport Commissioner) to formulate their new system.

During the whole process of replacing the old paper licence with smart card driving licence in Gujarat, challenges were many—starting from concept to application level. The biggest of all was the change management implementation for the government employees as well as for the users. This chapter describes the problems with the earlier paper-based licence system, how this innovative idea of smart card-based driving licence was introduced and its advantages including the cost-benefit comparison.

The Context

India, having been crossed a billion population, claims to be one of the largest economies by 2020. It still possesses 40 percent illiterate citizens and most of them are living below poverty line. The multi-lingual and multi-cultural general population, deep rooted in their traditions, does not provide welcoming environment for the introduction of a reformative system with IT applications. The common law system in its post-independent five decades has not undergone many changes to suit the working environment of free India. This has constantly encouraged increase in manipulation of the system for vested advantages. Thus, the society is put to sustained loss, as the regulatory mechanism does not possess abilities to challenge such manipulative forces. But, it is the human nature to invent new systems and technologies in different fields that keep changing the day-to-day life.

The 20th century is marked by technological rampage and dramatic cross-fertilization of scientific efforts that lead to unexpected breakthroughs. Maximum innovations have been made in the field of information technology (IT) and mass communication. The introduction of 'smart card-based driving licence' in Gujarat is one such example. Smart card—as the name suggests—is a card that is embedded with either a micro-processor and a memory chip or only a memory chip with non-programmable logic. The most common smart card applications are computer security systems, credit cards, banking, electronic cash, wireless communication and government identification. Application of smart card for a driving licence was mainly created to control issues related to duplicate licences and corrupt practices, which turned out to be a great success and changed the whole working environment in the transport department of Gujarat government.

Requirement for a driving licence

The Motor Vehicles Act, 1988 authorizes the Regional Transport Officer to issue driving licence to persons above 18 years of age and qualify the driving test. The Central Motor Vehicles Rules,

1989 prescribe the qualification required to obtain driving licence for various categories of vehicles. Normally, driving licences are classified according to the engine capacities of two-wheelers, light motor vehicles, heavy motor vehicles, and other specialized vehicles like cranes etc. The licence is issued first up to forty years of age and later it is renewed every five years based on medical check-up of the concerned person. Provisions for revocation of licence on grounds of disease or disability have been made in the Act. The licence may be suspended or cancelled if a person is convicted of an offence punishable under specified sections. Disqualification of a licence for a period is also possible under certain offences.

It is to be noted that the management of transport sector is a state subject. The state governments, with the support of the Central Motor Vehicles Act, formulate regulatory rules independently. Hence, applications of the provisions to monitor different activities of the transport sector may vary from state to state. The need for effective system of issuing and monitoring of driving licence is beyond argument as the rate and number of road accidents in India as well as in Gujarat has remained relatively high over time (Figure 2.1 and Table 2.1).

Figure 2.1

Persons affected by road accidents in Gujarat

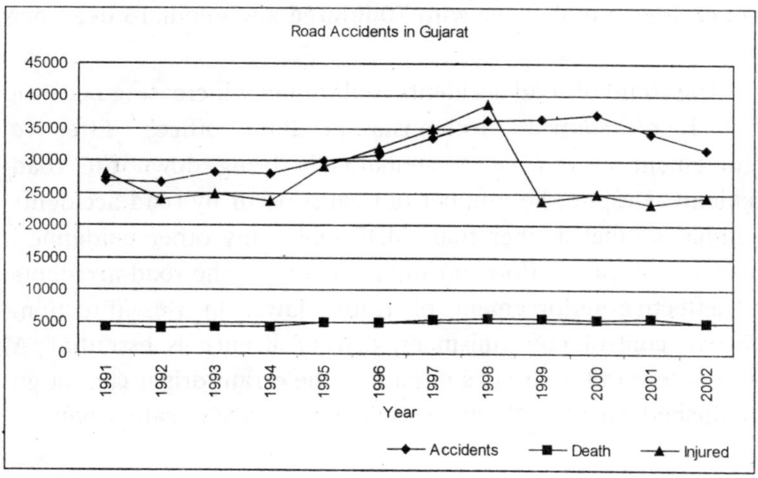

Table 2.1
Road accidents in Gujarat

Year	*Total number of accidents*	*Killed*	*Injured*	*Total number of vehicles*	*Vehicles growth from last year*
1995	29984	4800	29100	30,21,166	10%
1996	30975	4971	32143	33,77,798	12%
1997	33694	5328	35044	37,76,973	12%
1998	36300	5461	38806	42,03,473	11%
1999	36451	5479	23860	46,79,793	11%
2000	37132	5418	24924	51,90,732	11%
2001	34411	5571	23297	55,76,040	7%
2002	31941	4914	24467	60,07,969	8%

Source: Transport Department, Government of Gujarat (Vehicles Growth) and Central Road Research Institute, Road Accidents in Gujarat State, 2002.

The Central Road Research Institute, New Delhi reported in August 2004 that earthquakes and cyclones do not come every year but road accidents routinely come and 80,000 people (a year) in India simply get wiped out. It has been further reported that most of the accidents happened because of the drivers' negligence. In a state like Gujarat, during the last five years, about 100 road accidents took place with 70 injured and about 15 dead per day.

The trend of road accidents is alarmingly increasing because of lack of control mechanism at RTO offices. Effective enforcement of law can systematically bring down the road accidents. Despite the number of deaths occur by road accidents in India is much higher than AIDS or by any other epidemics, there is no serious effort to campaign against the road accidents and effective enforcement of traffic laws. In this direction, effective control mechanism on drivers' licence is essential. A sense of fear in the driver's mind that the errant driver cannot go unpunished was thought as the only way to ensure safe driving.

On an average, 800 drivers licences were issued per day prior to the introduction of smart card driving licence in the state. As of March 2004, about 8,000,000 licences are recorded in the register. However, there is no register for suspended or cancelled licences. Very often, the inspector takes the licences away when there is a major road accident to produce before the court of law. These licences are treated as cancelled. But, there is no register to compile and monitor such cancelled licences. Hence, effective control and monitoring of such large numbers of licences is only possible only through an ICT-based system.

Paper licence and its disadvantages

The paper licence is a pocket-size booklet having a few pairs of pages designed to carry information about the licence holder, description of vehicles the licence holder is permitted to drive, validity period, details of renewal and two pages for endorsement by the court. Often, the information is illegible. A number of signatures are put that are also illegible. A photograph repeatedly rubber-stamped, rarely strike similarity to the licence holder (Figure 2.2).

The way the system was operational was beset with severe inherent limitations. Misuse and abuse of the system was wide-spread. As the system is not foolproof it could not arrest delays,

Figure 2.2

Paper driving licence

manipulations and corruption. The state also used to lose revenue. A brief account of these flaws has been presented in the following sub-sections:

Ledgers and registers

To record the licence holders' address and validity period in a date-wise serial number, ledgers and registers are maintained at the Regional Transport Offices. However, for wrongful gain, transporters corrupt the employees to leave some lines of the ledgers unfilled to accommodate errant driver's expired licence valid in case of accident insurance claims etc. Such intentional mistakes to make invalid licences valid simply by entering the names in the ledger on a date prior to the licence expiry date meant to wrongfully benefit the transporter for fraudulent insurance claims.

Easy to forge

As outlined above, the paper licence is such that it is easy to make fake or forge a licence. It does not require great technical talent to manipulate it. In fact, there are many illegal outlets operating in many towns and cities where agents would supply instant driving licences without any medical certificate or driving test at a suitable cost depending on the place of issue asked for! The rubber stamps are put indiscriminately everywhere so as to make the handwritten information illegible. A number of illegible but coloured ink signatures are also put. The rubber stamp can be of Silchar in Arunachal Pradesh or of Dimapur in Nagaland, but a customer could get the licence instantly. There are also cases wherein a driver on highways possessing two or three such licences! These come in handy in case the previous one expires, gets stolen or to meet with any other such exigencies.

Susceptible to manipulation

In case of insurance claims in road accidents, it is necessary that the driver has a valid licence. Many times, because of carelessness or over-confidence, the drivers fail to renew the licence. This automatically leads to ineligibility of insurance claims. But, the drivers, using fake driving licences with the help of an employee in RTO office who, at a price proportionate to the insurance claim, makes a licence renewal entry in the office ledger. As a practice, to meet with such contingencies, the RTO employees leave one or two lines blank between two entries at random without recording any serial number. This symbiotic relation mutually benefits the corrupt employee and the careless driver. The employees as well as the errant drivers go unpunished because there is no effective control mechanism to catch such corrupt employee or errant driver.

Lack of control mechanism

Earlier, as the system was manual, it was impossible to record all traffic offences. It was too cumbersome to trace past offences, whenever recorded. Further, the RTO office systems did not have traffic offence computing system at the state level. As a result, many offences went without penalty or punishment.

There have also been cases when the judicial courts punish the drivers and issue orders to cancel their licences. Fake licences, from different states, come in handy as solutions to errant drivers. These fake licences could not be traced because of the lengthy inter-state paper correspondences. Poor record-keeping in most of the Regional Transport Offices comfortably help the drivers as inter-state and inter-district communications are not replied for months together. Unless a particular officer is persistent about a case, it is impossible to get the facts. The non-availability of facts and delay lead to poor control mechanism. Hence, the system becomes ineffective.

Genesis of smart card licence

Given rampant abuse of the system it was necessary to search for an effective alternative. The system should be foolproof, tamper-proof, secured, speedy and act as a deterrent. It should enable off-line communication.

A business magazine carried an article about the arrival of smart card technology way back in June 1998. The author had been facing the problem of excessive manipulations in driving licence. The paper-based driving licence could be easily forged to claim hefty insurance payments and other misuses. This article triggered the idea to make a memory chip with the dynamic and frozen data. That is how, the smart card technology was leveraged to have an effective and fully secured identification-based driving licence.

The smart card-based applications were getting popular in the western parts of the world since last one decade. Few countries had also experimented in introducing smart card for the driving licences. Building on these, the Gujarat government decided to design and develop an integrated driving licence system based on smart cards. Introduction of biometric identification was a major innovation in the system and this happened to be the first in the world.

Devising such solution is easier said than done. Work culture deep rooted in a society, which accepts 'bad practices' as a way of life, is likely to resist innovations, whatsoever good. Further, the uphill task was to make the society accept any new system. Some efforts to streamline the administration, strict enforcement and vigilance do improve the situation to an extent. Suspension or dismissal of an errant employee does not necessarily assure improved implementation of regulation. It cannot be guaranteed that the employee replaced against a dismissed one would be better than the earlier one. Often, it is seen that the suspended employee punishes the society doubly once reinstated back. It is also difficult to produce evidence against the corrupt employee, as system is inherently deficient. Needless to mention that sabotage at each stage was to be anticipated. It is expected that the vested interests repeatedly attempt to stop the process of introduction of any new system.

Being the first of its kind to be developed, it was also easy to raise doubts about the feasibility. A vague concept of smart card-based driving licence was very difficult to explain and detail out a fully secured system in the absence of same application elsewhere. Hence, designing a system and evolving procurement process, particularly in a hierarchical government system, was a tough task. Prima facie, there was a need to justify replacing the paper licences with the smart card-based driving licences. They pose a challenge to anyone who wants to bring reforms and enforce rule of law. Eventually efforts were put to leverage information technology to streamline the driving licence system. This is how, the introduction of smart card-based driving licence system was made in the state of Gujarat in India with integrated electronic monitoring system since 18th January, 1999.

The smart card technology

Since last one decade the smart card technology has been in use for a few other applications. Like computers, there are different cards depending on the application requirements. Over the time, smart cards are used particularly when there is a need for strong authentication of users or applications, mobility of vital information requiring protection or strong security and key management.

The smart card-based driving licence system in Gujarat has been designed jointly by the Office of the Transport Commissioner, M/s Smart Chip Ltd., New Delhi and ORGA of Germany. A smart card is essentially a plastic card complying with ISO 7810 and containing one (or more) Integrated Circuit (IC). These IC cards are able to store as well as verify information according to its programming.

System functions of a smart card

For the whole smart card system to work in harmony, there are various levels at which it functions. It can be explained as back office data management, applications, life cycle and open card platforms.

Back office data management

- *Input/output management:* It is a software component that needs to be decided at the stage of the system design itself. The input and output exchanges and the transaction protocol need to be finalized at this stage. Volume of data need to be transacted and stored in the chip and in the system are estimated and accordingly the system is designed.

- *Data management:* Tracking files and data from the directories created and processing the required transaction from the data obtained and integrating from any new input sourced to meet the objective results. If files need to be tagged, then this should be done at the design stage itself.
- *Security-related functions:* Predetermine algorithms, key generations and key management issues at the design stage itself.
- *Application generic functions:* Other major issues need to be considered at this stage are cardholder verification method (password) and electronic purse management.

Types of applications in smart card system design

Various applications based on off-line transactions and foolproof authentication can be designed as per the application requirement. Some examples of applications are as follow:

- Payment specific operations
  - Debit
  - Credit
  - Read balance
- Financial risk management
  - Generate application certificate
  - Get processing options
- Authentication
  - Run authentication
  - Generate signature

Smart card life cycle

At the stage of manufacturing itself the security aspects are covered. The confidentiality is very high because the chip itself generates its own unique PIN to identify with the system, which is designed to match the application. The precise life cycle of the smart card is as follows:

- *Manufacturing:* A unique serial number is written in the chip during manufacturing.
- *Initialization:* Permanent applications are loaded in the chip.
- *Personalization:* Information related to the specific cardholder is loaded.
- *Applications:* Applications can update their information, new applications can be downloaded, old may be removed.
- *End-of-life:* Because the plastic ages quite quickly, the card technology and the security are improved from time to time, smart cards are often replaced every two or three years with new security systems.

Open card platforms

One smart card can have many applications that can be online or off-line. Smart card is convenient to carry. Secured accessibility to personalized services for more than one can be provided on the basis of biometric or equivalent security authentication. The factors listed below illustrate the need for open platforms in the smart card applications:

- Moving from card issuance to application issuance:
  - One card can contain many applications.
- Interoperability worldwide is nearly impossible:
  - Instead of having one standardized application, it is much easier to have a standard way of loading an application in all cards and then adapt to circumstances (e.g., download local application).
- Development cycle time was incompatible with the time to market required for most applications.
- Once the infrastructure or readers and cards are in place, it becomes possible to download in cards new services and new applications easily and quickly.

Database management system (DBMS)

As mentioned earlier, the smart card-based driving licence system was the first of its kind in the world. Further, this was the first biometrics identification used in the world for any licencing system. This innovation needs boldness. Particularly in India, thinking of such innovation itself is an act of bravery and perhaps well ahead of time. Since the elected government was keen to replace corruption-prone paper-based driving licence system, the smart card driving licence system could be designed by using a memory chip. The biometric identification system requires huge storage space, as every fingerprint may need about 750 kilobytes. Hence, originally, it was designed to use DB2 (RDBMS). However, on account of minor commercial dispute, RDBMS had to be changed to Oracle '9i' after a year.

Optimize back-end configurations

Because of biometric identification, the system was in need of larger capacity to store and update data on a regular basis. For every fingerprint, about 750 kilobytes are required whereas the memory chip has only 1 kilobyte capacity. Hence, the fingerprint identification system was designed in such a way that the system creates its own unique templates within 250 bytes and identifies. These templates are then encrypted in the chip, which would enable the database to match "one" to "one" after identifying name, address and other personal details. This is how the system is optimized to cross-check the data from "1" to "1" fingerprint. Introduction of biometrics as identification tool was a major innovation in the system.

However, the network capability is restricted because of 64 kbps telephone leased line connectivity. Hence, it is impossible to transact speedy and voluminous data.

Capture transactions electronically

Since it was the first of its kind in the world to have biometric identification, the security of the system was not greatly threatened. All relevant data are captured and stored electronically. Moreover, any manipulation of security system would not yield sizeable gain to anyone. Therefore, all electronic transactions are fully secured and the system is designed to create its own PIN and unique identification templates (32-bit encryption).

Biometric data as security

Gujarat in India has become the first authority in the world to introduce smart card driving licence project with fingerprint biometric stored on the card.[1] The use of biometrics has been recognized as one of the most secure means of identification and authentication. Fingerprint authentication of the individual has been undertaken to ensure that only authentic licences are issued. This system virtually eliminates issuing of more than one licence to a person. As the card contains the fingerprints of licence-holder, the same card can be used for other applications as well.

The biometric is the identification of a person using one-dimensional data, usually collected in an uncontrolled environment applying sensors and transmission lines of uncertain characteristics. Fingerprint is one such identification tool emerging as standardized biometric identification from the available biometric recognitions. There are three approaches to fingerprint matching by digital computers: (1) transform; (2) correlation; and (3) minutiae. Transform methods, perhaps based on the 2-dimensional FFT (Fast Fourier Transform) to find the amplitudes of the equally-spaced frequencies. Given the variation of a single fingerprint from one image to the next, it is hard to believe that 'global' transform methods could be refined enough to reliably recognize fingerprints over the wide variety of conditions encountered. Correlation methods have been used by a number of vendors. The idea is to 'overlay' two fingerprints to see if they match. Because of their variability, one cannot overlay the

1. Biometric Technology Today (April 1999), Volume 7 No. 1, SJB Research, Longport, U.K. http:/www.sjbresearch.com

Figure 2.3

Biometric Technology Today declaring Gujarat as the first authority in the world to use biometric identification

Btt™

biometric technology today

sjb research

April 1999 • Volume 7 Number 1

Company News

Inside this issue...

02 News — Netherlands pilots signature verification programme

02 News — API unified but template question remains unresolved

03 News — Brazilian integrator likely to develop biometric market

03 News — Test results favour use of ultrasound technology

03 News — Indian state pioneers biometric smart card driving licence

04 News — Trust is needed for e-commerce growth, says US survey

05 News in brief — All the rest of the news, including Mission Data Systems and Biometric Access Corporation rescind purchase agreement,

05 Mytec adds a physical access control reader to Touchstone and 3GI designs security and access control plan for US Bureau of Diplomatic Security

06 Forthcoming events — Details of nine industry events over the next eight months, including Bio '99, *Btt*'s own two-day conference/exhibition preceded by a one-day workshop

07 Survey — Payment systems — banking and welfare: In a dual survey *Btt* outlines the areas in which biometric technologies are being used to secure payment systems. Plus a detailed listing of banking and welfare payment systems worldwide

12 Backchat — Rumours, snippets and quotable quotes heard during *Btt*'s rounds of the industry...

Comment from the Editor

The Indian State of Gujarat's choice of a biometric driving licence *(see p3)* is encouraging at a time when public support for the use of biometric technology for licensing has waned in countries such as the USA. The US market for biometric licensing is unlikely to grow beyond the five states already using the technology, because of growing protests against the use of personal identifiers such as biometrics and social security numbers on publicly issued documents. The recent attempts by some states to profit from the sale of personal data such as photographs has only fuelled public cynicism about the misuse of personal data. The International Biometric Industry Association's clear statement of privacy principals could not have been better timed *(see side bar, p2)*.

Standards issues are being clarified too. There has always been uncertainty about the viability of standardising templates because of their vendor proprietary content. Speculation has centred on whether the proprietary nature was inherent to the content or just somehow descriptive of it. It might be worth remembering that there was concern and disagreement over the original notion of a generic biometric API because of this proprietary principle: the unification of APIs ends this concern.

Time has either clarified that it is not an issue, or the burden of the problem has shifted to the more specific issue of biometric templates. Treating templates as an independent standardisation issue may then deliver the first considered opinion of where the boundary between common and proprietary technology lies. However, this must be married to a solution that users and developers can anticipate as manageable and upgradable in their applications — and some thought should certainly be given to customers' needs.

Calum Bunney

entire prints, but can overlay small, selected portions of the prints from areas assessed to be of 'good quality'. Using such overlays, it is possible to even match the pores along the ridges of a high-resolution fingerprint image.

Most vendors use minutiae-based systems that identify the ridge endings and 'bifurcations' (splits) in the prints. The location of these minutiae and the angle of the ridge at the point of their occurrence are compared to those of other prints to determine a match. It is presumed that two images from the same finger will not be exactly the same, so the comparison algorithms allow for movement and rotation of the finger, stretching between minutiae, and missing minutiae points. But, for digital fingerprinting, it is commonly acceptable that minutiae matching and the same is taken for this system.

Record-keeping and monitoring

Smart card-based driving licence is designed primarily with an idea that there is a foolproof control mechanism for issuing and managing the driving licence in the state. Further, the government can also create interface with other applications like citizen card, ration card, health card, etc. The interface deals with other states and other service providers also, and it becomes easier since the driving licence law is the same for all the states of India. This flexibility in management is a major advantage in bringing in smart card-based driving licence system.

Smart cards do not need online connectivity. The battery-operated handheld terminals issued to enforcement staff for on-road checking are adequate to read and update the status. The enforcement staff through the handheld terminals can verify the past history of a licence holder. When a licence holder is caught committing an offence, the enforcement staff inserts the smart driving licence into the terminal and verifies the offender's past history. The degree of penalty can then be made variable. A provision to cancel the licence if a person exceeds a said number of offences is also being incorporated. A 'chalan' is generated through an inbuilt printer in the terminal. The records are stored both in the card as well as in the terminal.

At the end of the day, the data accumulated on the terminal are downloaded onto a PC at the RTO. The update list of offenders is thus available almost instantly, which in the past would have been impossible to gather. Thus, the system will help in bringing positive values to the driving population, which is the need of the time.

Central monitoring system

In addition to the above, a central monitoring system has been created for streamlining the entire licence and driver-related issues. Some of the salient features of the system are:

- Daily report generation
  - Number of new licences issued
  - Duplicate licences issued
  - Total offences
- Offence recording held on terminals and downloading on server
- Automatic licence cancellation
- Fingerprint storage for security
- Duplicate licence retrieval through finger print verification
- Fingerprint matching with central database before a new licence is issued
- Hot listing of licence
- Penalty collection data

The enrolment process

Given the advantages of smart cards offer, the system was designed to be convenient and easy. The data capture and issue of the licence are processed in a single window clearance system. All Regional Transport Offices are equipped with smart card personalization system, which consists of a PC, smart card printer, fingerprint capture device, video camera, and signature tablet and customized software. This enables an end-to-end process capture.

The whole process of getting a licence has been simplified. Now, a person has to just walk into the issue centre and walk out with a licence.

Figure 2.4

Data capture and personalization of the system

Step 1: Photograph

Details of the applicant are fed into a PC located at the counter. Simultaneously, the photograph of the person is taken through the camera.

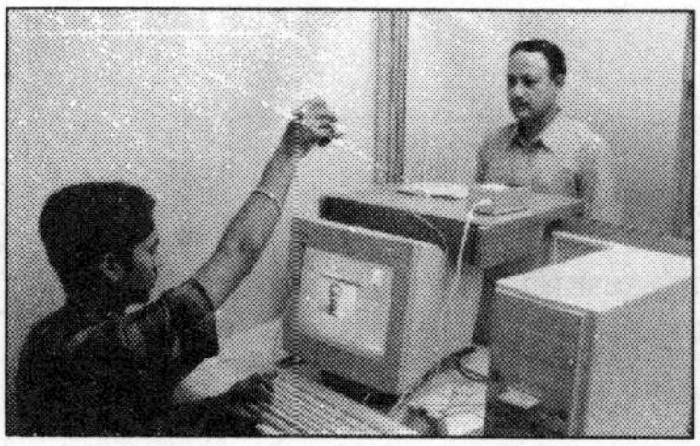

Step 2: Fingerprint captured and recorded

After that the applicant's fingerprints are captured through a fingerprint scanner and stored in the database. The system is also designed to generate templates of the fingerprints and store them on the chip because of memory limitations.

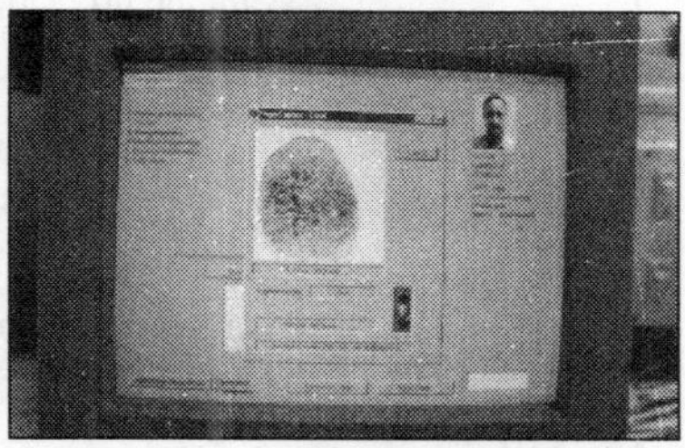

Step 3: Signature

The signature of the licence holder is also captured electronically through the signature table on which the applicant needs to sign.

Step 4: Capturing and delivering

Once all details of the applicant are captured, with customized licence issuing software, the card is printed on the smart card printer. The details are also stored electronically on the chip. The entire process, complicated as it may sound, takes only a few minutes and is characterized by its ease of operation. It should be noted that security has been given a prime importance and the whole operation is performed under high-security conditions.

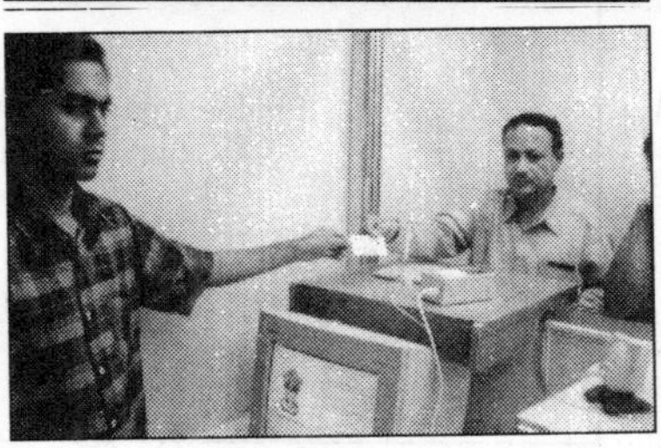

Figure 2.5

Issuing of smart card-based driving licence

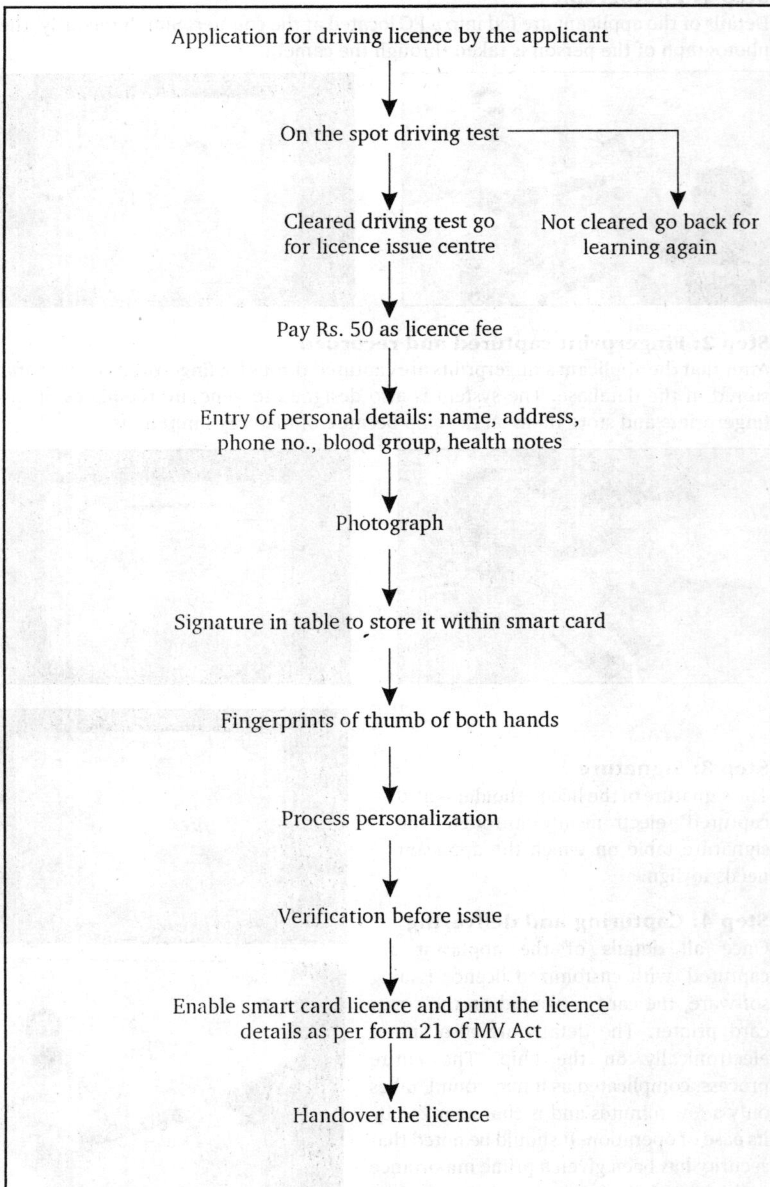

Benefits

Since the driving licence is universally accepted as an identity card, the security features deserve highest importance. Smart card performs specific functions that are 'programmed' for the card issuer and to enable transactions to be captured and processed, the card is inserted into a terminal device. The smart card, therefore, offers the remarkable combination of being secure, mobile and unique (cannot be duplicated), and is currently the only available cost-effective alternative to achieve an open, flexible, yet safe transaction-processing environment.

Thus, for transactions processed under the smart card environment, all the parties involved, viz., the card issuer and the user are sure that the transaction is totally protected against fraud. With the use of smart card technology, not only is there an elimination of fraud, but there is also the added convenience due to the mobility of the card.

Figure 2.6

Paper licence to smart card licence

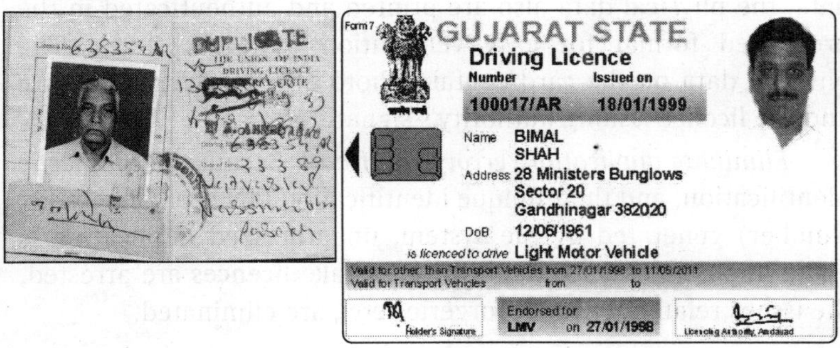

Smart cards have inherent advantages, which permit and necessitate its application in almost all spheres of daily life. These are:

- Latest technology
- Perform operations off-line
- Dynamic, mobile and secure

- User-friendly environment
- Secure and tamper-proof identity
- Eliminate duplication and fraud
- Long-lasting and durable physical and electronic record
- Capabilities can be added and extended
- Can be seamlessly linked to main computer networks

High security

Perhaps, the most significant feature of the smart card is its ability to store data in a highly 'secure' manner. This means that the smart card provides a high level of security to the user and the issuer. This security is available because of the "micro-chip", which allows certain data to be encrypted and stored only once so as to be "available" for reading only to an authorized person.

Certain areas of the card's memory can be 'fused' after storage, making alteration of its contents impossible. Being tamper-proof is thus one manifestation of it being 'Smart'.

Physical and electronic personalization: Besides electronic data, the physical data also are printed and authenticated in the prescribed format for easy verification by other states. The physical data on the card contain photo of the driver, signature and the licence issuing authority's signature.

Eliminate duplication, errors and fraud: Because of biometric identification, and their unique identification PIN (Personal Index Number) generated by the system, unauthorized duplication is made impossible. Once duplication or fake licences are arrested, the issues related to fraud, forgeries etc., are eliminated.

Data management easy

High data storage capacity: The smart card can store much larger volumes of data, than any other comparable media, such as the magnetic strip card. While the magnetic strip card usually stores around 200 bytes, the latest smart cards can be programmed to store more than 16,000 bytes, in separate logical files for different uses and applications. In addition to the storage capacity, smart card provides exceptionally long life to stored data—more than 10 years, and the card itself can be read/written more than 100,000 times.

Logical access to card data: Besides storing raw data, the smart card can also store the logic or conditions that are imposed by the issuer of the card, which apply to its use. Hence, the card itself controls its use and thus prevents misuse. This eliminates the need for an online network of any kind for this purpose.

Perform operations off-line: The major reason for failure of paper licence system was lack of effective and speedy communication between the inspectors to offices and within offices. Compilation of offences and monitoring them for effective enforcement of law was not possible because of this reason.

Keeping this in mind, the smart card driving licence memory chip was mapped in such a way that permanent information is only readable and the dynamic information like traffic offences are writable. Data deletion from the chip or from the MIS is authenticated only at the top level. Hence, lower-level officers cannot add or delete offences. The information stored in the chip can be downloaded from the reader and MIS is updated daily.

Reduce network dependence: The system is designed in a way that the handheld readers do not depend on the network for highway operations. The traffic offences are recorded in the chip as well as in the reader. The reader is designed to download this recorded information for database updating. This off-line offence monitoring system greatly reduces the dependence of network connectivity.

Dynamic and mobile

Because of its light weight, slight flexibility and temperature proof etc., the smart card licence is designed to withstand rain and heat up to 100 degree centigrade. Besides, it is easy to carry, and in case of loss, it is fully secured because no one else can use it. It is mapped in such a way that the traffic offences can be added and deleted. However, the system is designed to suspend the licence automatically once the holder commits fine offences. Hence, its capabilities are designed in such a way that it can be added and extended.

Convenient to use: The smart card is thus highly convenient both to the holder of the card as well as to the issuer. The size of the card is the same as the conventional credit card, and can be printed and embossed with all kinds of images, holograms and pictures. The plastic itself is weatherproof and long-lasting.

Figure 2.7

Smart driving licence system

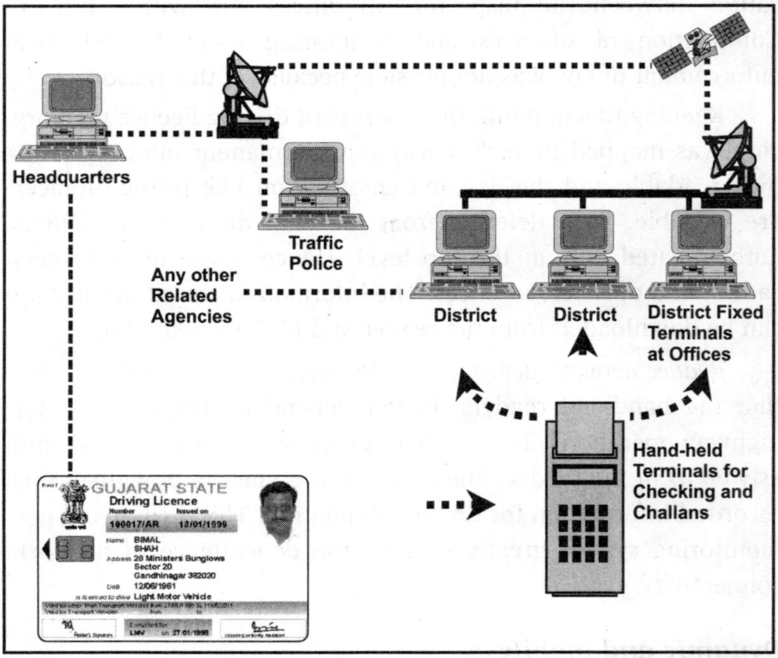

User-friendly features

Personal details: The personal details like name, address and telephone numbers, etc., are not only printed on the card, but also stored in the chip as well as in the system. The details of category of vehicles the licence holder is qualified to drive and the validity period is also printed as well stored in the chip. These details in the system cannot be changed unless authorized new card is issued.

Medical details: The memory chip is mapped to carry the health conditions, allergic details to drugs or any other medicine and blood group details etc. These particulars are recorded on voluntary basis of the licence holders. These parts of 250 bytes are mapped in such a way that additions and deletions are possible.

Easy to use/handle: Because of its lightweight design, similar to bank credit cards, it is easy to carry for the holder. On the other hand, the handheld readers given to traffic inspectors are also easy to operate, economical and require no elaborate training to use them. Thus, the whole system is designed to be user-friendly.

Effective enforcement: The paper-based licence system was not designed to have off-line instant access to the details of the licence holder. But, the memory chip carries the details of earlier traffic offences and this has helped to suspend the licence forthwith by the card itself once the offences are entered. This was not possible in the paper licence system and writing letters seeking information through postal communication used to take very long time. The new system is designed not only to read the licence on the road by readers but also suspend it instantly once the fifth traffic offence is committed on the road. The licence holder cannot drive further once the fifth offence is recorded. The recorded details of penalty collected are downloaded to the system once the inspector reaches the office. The system was primarily designed user-friendly not only to the holders but to the regulators who can effectively enforce the law. A decline in the rate of road accidents has also been observed after the introduction of smart card licence since 1999 (Figure 2.1). However, the system does not operate to its potential because of training needs of RTO and police personnel.

Immediate retrieval of data: In case of paper licence it was not possible to retrieve data once damaged due to termites or other reasons, which was a drawback for enforcing the law effectively. This was the key reason for insurance frauds, and traffic offenders being repeatedly motivated to commit offences.

The driving licence MIS was designed in such a way that once in 24 hours all information is updated to the central system located in RTO, Ahmedabad through 64 kbps telephone leased line network connectivity. After successful conversion of data into DBMS, the system can provide immediate information about any driving licence holder of Gujarat in any of the RTO office.

One-stop shop: Obtaining driving licence in paper-based system was an ordeal to a common citizen. At the same time, if one spends money, it was also possible to get the licence without giving a driving test through the agents. In smart card system, every person needs to go to Regional Transport Office and go through enrolment process wherein two fingerprints are recorded for instant issue of driving licence. This one-stop shop eliminated the corrupt practices of agent-inspector nexus.

Cost benefit

At the time of implementation cost estimated for whole system was Rs. 361 lakhs. However, against 250 personalization units, only 172 units in 25 districts were installed at the final cost of Rs. 257 lakhs. This cost includes 192 handheld terminals to read smart card driving licences on the road for off-line checking.

One smart card licence cost was fixed at Rs. 50 which includes personalization and operations. The ownership of hardware, software and DBMS was agreed to be with the Commissioner of Transport from the installation itself. The licence fee of Rs. 50 is collected by the RTO office to comply the legality of fee collection and the same is transferred to M/s Smart Chip at the end of every month. It was agreed that the licences would be issued on all working days in all centres and there was no minimum level of daily, weekly or monthly card issuance stipulated.

After the introduction of the smart card driving licence system, applicants find it very easy and simple to come and carry out on the spot driving test and get smart card licence issued then and there. Once the driving test is complete, the licences issuance process takes about two minutes. Larger urban centres are equipped with ten personalization units.

Table 2.2
Comparisons between paper and smart licences

Earlier - Paper Licence	*Now - Smart Card*
Transport is a state subject. There does not exist a central control mechanism.	With help of smart card, central monitoring system at the state level is possible.
The previous driving licence did not provide foolproof identification system.	Foolproof.
Manipulation of the system for vested advantages was easy.	List out offenders instantly.
Driving licence regulation was the only way to improve the situation.	Effective for enforcing the laws.
No effective control mechanism to catch the corrupt practices.	Have deterrent effect.
Old paper driving licence were easy to forge or fake.	Almost impossible to forge the smart card-based driving licence with biometric identification.
Design of the old licence with rubber stamp on it was very easy to duplicate and sale by the agents (corruption very high).	Low chances of corruption.
Pocket size booklet, inconvenient to carry.	Tamper-proof, easy to carry.
Long delayed paper-based communication.	Communicate off-line.
Illegal agents extort applicants.	On the spot issuance of licence at Rs. 50 only.
Increased road accidents.	Reduced road accident rates despite steep increase of vehicles.

Earlier, to get a paper licence, it used to cost an applicant more than Rs. 1,000 because illegal agents extract more money from the applicants as if to help them and would send the licence to the given address after two or more months.

Constraints

The positive aspect of implementation of the smart card driving licence technology is that a system has been built which provides opportunity to improve upon in the future. But, still, there are certain issues that restrict it to be a fully successful technology. These are:

- It is essential that the government supports such innovative project like this and the unflinching such support only can create a force for project approval, resources allocation and procurement procedures and implementation in time.
- Selecting a right kind of vendor for implementation.
- Managerial and training needs are yet to be fully attended to.
- Designed automatic control and enforcement mechanisms are not fully operational.
- The state plans to convert all the existing paper licences of about 10 million to smart card driving licences in about 24 months, which is only possible with adequate and trained staff.
- It was planned to procure more than one thousand handheld terminals for on-road checking and connected with the central monitoring system for automatic suspension of licence if a driver found committed five traffic offences. But, this could not be done.

Conclusion

Gujarat has taken a lead in the successful implementation of this revolutionary technology. There has not only been a streamlining in the functioning of the department, but the resources are being utilized in a more optimal way. This system would be of immense benefit if adopted nationally. Finally, smart cards are:

- Foolproof
- Flexible
- Master Identification Card for citizens
- Interface—other applications
- Interface—other states
- Interface—other service providers

These are greater benefits that can be derived by adopting this technology in other realms of life as well. The World Smart Card Forum and many international governments appreciated the introduction of smart card driving licence with biometric identification. The Surface Transport Ministry, Government of India plans to replicate the project in other states. Special care need to be exercised in developing specifications and procurement process, else it may invite unscrupulous forces to distort the system. An attempt to develop a uniform national level system, considering the volume of data transactions involved and absence of network capabilities appears difficult.

3

Automation of Inter-State Border Transport Check-Posts

Transport sector is a major revenue contributor to the state government exchequer. As expected, like all revenue contributing sectors, this sector too had been burdened with all the inefficiencies and was accompanied by the culture of corruption. Having successfully implemented a smart card-based driving licence with biometric identification and proved to be the leader in e-governance reforms in the country, the transport department of the Government of Gujarat decided to explore other potential avenues of e-governance applications. The state implemented e-governance applications in the form of a fully automated inter-state border checks-posts in 1999.

The system was designed in-house to suit various activities like issue of driving licence through 1.2 kb memory chip smart card, registration of vehicles through hybrid smart card with 1.5 mb optical medium and 4 kb micro-processor chip card and automation of inter-state border check-posts by installing 58 computerized electronic weigh bridges with an online video monitoring system at the head office. The introduction of these information technology (IT) applications has led to speedier and transparent transactions of governmental activities. The initiative also helped in curbing corrupt practices. This has resulted in increased revenue realization from the motor vehicle tax and penalty collected from overloaded vehicles. Compared to the investment of Rs. 185 million to implement this project, the income expected at sustainable level is around Rs. 3,000 million per annum once the total integration is completed. Further, it is expected to enhance the revenue collected at the field offices by providing online transactional information that would form the backbone of tax revenue MIS. This chapter describes the system, as it existed before and after the implementation of the project and its benefits. A detailed account of implementation process of the project has also been presented.

The Motor Vehicle Act, 1988 provides for the levy of entry tax on transport motor vehicles entering in the state of Gujarat. As per the Act, the tax is levied on every entry in the state of a motor transport vehicle plying under a permit granted under the Motor Vehicle Act, 1988 by an authority having jurisdiction outside the state. The motor vehicle tax is to be paid by the operator of the commercial/motor transport vehicle in cash. In addition, collection of penalties for overloading, issue of permit to operate commercial transport activities for a temporary period etc., also form part of the system.

Gujarat shares borders with the states of Maharashtra, Madhya Pradesh and Rajasthan. There are 10 inter-state check-posts. The trunk line connecting Mumbai and Delhi passes through the state. About 30,000 vehicles enter the state every day. About 80 percent of them are commercial transport vehicles. Of these, about 70 percent are overloaded beyond the permissible limit to the extent of 2.5 to 4 tonnes. In addition, the state has about 6,37,292 commercial transport vehicles operating by March 2004, within the state. These vehicles cross the state border at least once a month. The check-posts were not adequately equipped with the capacity to handle such high volume of traffic.

Pre-project situation

The check-posts function as major activity centres in implementation of the Motor Vehicle Act, 1988. In the pre-project situation, the check-posts were managed manually. In addition to collecting motor vehicle tax, the other important activities, undertaken at the check-posts, were:

- Collection of composite tax and composition fine
- Issue of temporary permit to transport vehicles
- Collection of departmental actions
- Issue of overloading tokens
- Maintenance of different registers
- Preparation of various MIS reports
- Daily cash depositing in bank

In carrying out these activities, the manual system was totally inadequate. The processes and the resultant problems have been summarized below:

Slow vehicle clearance

All the check-posts located near the border were having a single-wide lane or two-lane width. The location of some of the check-posts was on the shoulder of the road, which further narrowed the width. Each commercial vehicle entering the state was to be verified for their compliance with Motor Vehicle Act, 1988 and Bombay Motor Vehicle Act. The operator is expected to stop the vehicle and handover the following documents for verification:

- RC book
- National permit, if any
- In case permit is not available, a temporary permit has to be obtained
- Checking report (CR) and departmental action case
- Receipt of cash payment

The data elements verified are:

- Motor vehicle number
- Vehicle type and class
- Permissible load
- Actual load carried
- Permit number
- Type of offence (departmental action cases taken by any Regional Transport Office)
- Fees/fine/tax amount

These procedures meant that each vehicle had to stop and show all the documents at the counter. If suspected, the inspector may physically inspect the vehicle for its content and quantity. This arrangement would mean clearance of only one vehicle at a time. It used to take about 20 to 30 minutes to check and clear one vehicle. With limited number of officers verifying, backlog grew and queues became longer. Sometimes it took days before the clearance was given to vehicle as some cases involve communication with central office for permits also. The unduly long procedure to check the tax papers and confirming with the respective registering authority leads to forceful detention of the vehicles for number of days. The manual process thus was a seedbed for the growth of corrupt practices and evasion of taxes. In turn, it became even more cumbersome for those wanting to abide by the law and unwilling to resort to unethical practice. This also meant slowing down of flow of other traffic.

As the pace of vehicle clearance was slow, it was not possible for verifying all the vehicles. Even in cases where vehicles were checked, given the pressure on clearing the vehicle fast, the checking was inadequate. In case of the check-posts in the state, it was observed that only half of the transport vehicles held valid permit. Many of the vehicles carried forged permit documents. This system perpetuated illegal operation of vehicles as well as movement of prohibited goods.

Overloading of the vehicles

The transport law was enacted many decades ago. No major changes in the law have been made to match the automobile's growth rate. Transport is a state subject. Different states have adopted different standards. Permitted loads by vehicle type vary from state to state. Some states allow vehicles to carry 52 metric tonnes as against the generally authorized load of 32 metric tonnes by Indian Motor Vehicle Act. Hence, there is a rush to buy and register transport vehicles in those states. Even though this practice is not desirable, so far suitable amendments in the law to fix uniform loading capacity has not been possible. In the absence of uniform legal framework, it is very difficult to prevent corrupt practices. During the course of design of the project, it was observed that more than 50 percent of transport vehicles did not hold valid permit for the goods they carried or they held forged permits/documents. Further, over 80 percent of the transport vehicles carried overloads. A vehicle, which has permission to carry 32 MT load, has been found carrying more than 58 MTs of steel rolls.

It is to be noted that the purpose of carrying overload for the transport vehicles is not to evade the road tax but excise duty or income tax. In industries/factories gate passes are issued for only permissible load, thus the industrial turnover is restricted in such a way that they can evade taxes for the overloaded part of production. Such overloads sustain on account of bad practices operative at the check-posts. By such kind of Act private individuals benefit but the society in general and the government in particular have to face several adverse impacts. It includes loss of revenue to the governments due to evasion of excise duty and income tax. Overloading also results in premature decay of the road surface and increase vehicular emissions leading to worsening air quality.

Employees security risk

About 8 to 10 thousand transport vehicles pass every day through inter-state border check-posts. Poorly staffed check-posts can hardly handle 100 vehicles per day because it has only put 4 or 5 inspectors for 3-shift duty including weekly breaks. This means 1.3 inspectors for an 8-hour shift are needed to check and clear 400 vehicles per hour. It is humanly not possible. Further, the pre-project cash collection of the check-posts in Gujarat used to be about Rs. 30 lakhs per day. This amount is kept in the check-posts itself. During the weekends, the collection of 3-4 days is kept in the check-posts. In spite of such high cash transactions, there was no official security force at the check-posts. Lack of such security lead to repeated violent incidents caused by unruly drivers during night hours.

To meet the situation, the inspectors themselves used to employ their own security personnel and supporting staff. These informal arrangements at the check-posts were found to be working well at a nominal illegal fee per tonnage collected from the overloaded vehicles at the entry of the state. These illegal collections as reported, may be in the order of a few lakhs of rupees in a single day. Because of such thriving income at the check-posts, inspectors try to get posted at the check-post. Assessments indicate that against the illegal earning of 100 rupees by the staff, the state was deprived of its legitimate revenue to the tune of 4,000 rupees.

The tenure of Transport Commissioner is generally about two to three years. It is difficult for the commissioner to understand the system, its problems, devise solutions and then implement corrective measures by a single officer against the collective wisdom of employees who are habituated to bad practices. Because of the sizeable monitoring influence, the department ultimately becomes a hub for politically motivated employee union activities. In such a working environment, there was very little room for system correction or effective supervision. The mindset of the employees was so strong that it always looked impossible to bring about any change in the system. Therefore, it was thought to use information technology (IT) as a tool to correct the system with a strategic approach by involving the transporters as well the employees in implementing the system right from the design stage.

The Project: Initiation to implementation

Stakeholders' involvement

The basic objective of full automation of all the 10 inter-state border check-posts is to establish an efficient and user-friendly system. At the beginning itself, it was clear that technology was possible to acquire, develop and utilize to its best effect. The major challenge was to change the mindsets of the employees and eradicate the all-pervasive culture of corruption. The process evolved over time and involved all employees in decision-making.

Building teams that perform

The total number of inter-state check-posts in Gujarat is 10. To start with, from amongst the employees, a leader was identified for each check-post based on the assessment of his credibility and ability to meet high-income targets. He was given adequate freedom to choose his team for manning the check-post. Daily reporting of income became a practice. He was given free access to communicate to the head of the department, i.e., the Commissioner of Transport. This increased the confidence level of the employees. Realizing that they are empowered and their performance is recognized, they derived a sense of satisfaction.

Creating a platform for stakeholders' participation

As a step forward, few members from those teams were picked up for weekly brainstorming sessions along with the transport association members to find a workable solution. These brainstorming sessions initially became a platform to trade charges, but later helped to develop a level of trust among the stakeholders, viz., inspectors, transporters and the Commissioner of Transport. To begin with, these discussions focused on the following objectives:

Figure 3.1

Location of inter-state check-posts

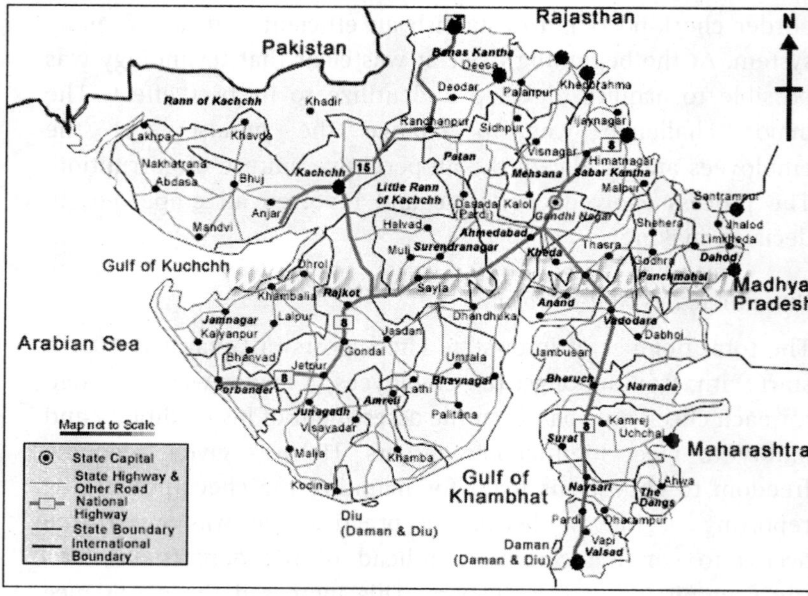

Shamlaji	12 lanes	Shamakhiali	6 lanes
Palanpur	6 lanes	Bhilad	12 lanes
Deesa	6 lanes	Songadh	6 lanes
Tharad	2 lanes	Dahod	6 lanes
Ambaji	2 lanes	Zalod	2 lanes

- To check 100 percent of the transport vehicles crossing inter-state border check-post in Gujarat
- Speedy operation and minimizing detention of vehicles
- Enhance compliance of law
- Adopting best practices in operation
- Prevent tax evasion
- Make the system user-friendly

It was envisaged that all transactions shall be recorded and create integrated databased management system.

Golden token system

The result of series of deliberations led to an innovation in the form of 'Golden Token System'. As per this system, a transporter could buy monthly tokens of Rs. 5,000, Rs. 3,000 and Rs. 2,000 for different load carrying capacity vehicles and these vehicles would not be stopped for checking by inspectors in the state. Successful introduction of Golden Token System also received criticism from a few other states stating that Gujarat was legalizing the overloading. But, the transporters were very happy because of reduced level of harassment on the highway. The uncertainty about the time duration taken to deliver the goods also greatly reduced, because once token is displayed on the wind screen, the vehicle should not be checked by an officer less than ARTO.

This system of communication and introduction of the Golden Token System generated a positive environment in dealings between the transporters and the inspectors. Now, they started sharing a common platform to innovate a new system for smooth functioning of the RTO check-posts. This communication channel created in the process, which was largely informal, between the stakeholders, played a vital role in changing the dynamics of system operation. This formed a base to carry forward with the task of building a fully automated computerized inter-state border check-posts by leveraging IT tools.

Moving forward with the idea of machines manning the check-posts

A core team was formed consisting of transporters association representatives, team leaders from various check-posts, and the Joint/Deputy Directors of the Transport Department to suggest operational reforms in the check-posts. This core team continued to review every fortnight about how to still make better effect of the Golden Token System. In one of such review meetings the author suggested that IT applications might ease the check-post clearance still faster and better. The idea of machines manning the check-posts was well received by the team. Minimizing the human interface in transacting with the vehicles was recommended by the team.

Once the team agreed to the concept, it started working on a strategy how to involve other stakeholders, like decision-makers in the government and the employees. It was thought to undertake a campaign about how good is golden token and how good would it be if machines man the check-posts. This campaign posed questions at various levels as to whether the idea was feasible? Would it work? The affirmative answers from the employees manning the check-posts and the policy makers from the government were encouraging. This motivated the team to carry forward with the next stage to work on designing a system. The fortnightly brainstorming sessions continued regularly with a purpose to update all stakeholders and get them involved in the implementation process and suggest new ideas and concepts.

By co-opting all the stakeholders through direct/indirect measures, a project proposal for approval to implement the fully computerized automation of the check-posts was sent to the state government. When this proposal reached the state government, the smart card driving licence system was already in place and had received wide publicity and appreciation from all over the world. In this light Government of Gujarat did not hesitate to implement the fully computerized automation of inter-state border check-posts.

Designing and implementation of the system

Once the system objectives were made known to all the stakeholders, the main features of the system could be evolved with the consultation process. The consultation process continued throughout the implementation period. Intensive consultations were carried out with the transporters' association members. Suggestions received from the transporters, during consultation process, were put up to the inspectors and other employees including the security personnel to analyze its workability.

Procurement procedures are the major reason for failure in implementing most of the government projects. First of all, the project should have a budget provision as a new item. It should also have administrative and financial approvals prior to commencement of implementation. Otherwise, the procedure involving stage-wise submission of procurement activities to various committees is lengthy and cumbersome. For an innovative project like this, to go through the process within one-year duration was a challenge! Such innovative projects, in addition to the lengthy and cumbersome procedure, also involve the risk of adverse publicity. Sometimes, the vested interests carry anti-project campaign with the help of the press or political leaders etc. This dissuades many enthusiastic officers venturing into such innovative projects. The challenges involved in implementation are many.

Selecting the vendor

Despite anticipating such criticisms and adverse environment, the team ventured into implementing the project by releasing a procurement advertisement “Seeking Total Solution for Fully Computerized Automation of Inter-state Border RTO Check-Posts” in June 1998. Pre-bid meetings were called in two stages at the interval of two weeks to explain the project details. About 20 bidders participated in the pre-bid meeting. They were encouraged to visit the check-posts, have free dialogue with the officers and seek information at any level before the closure of bids. The bidders sought 45 days’ time limit for final submission of bids, which was duly granted. Finally, eight bidders submitted their proposals.

Transparent bid process: Realizing the complexity and the associated risks involved and also to co-opt other collaborative departments, a committee of Secretaries of Roads & Buildings Department, Industry Department, Finance Department, Information Technology Department, Transport Department and the experts from IIM, Ahmedabad was formed to evaluate the proposal. The bidders were asked to make detailed presentation about the proposed total solution to the committee. The committee, after a detailed evaluation, shortlisted three bidders as qualified.

The shortlisted bidders were once again called for a briefing about the technical requirement of the total solution. The bidders with their representatives were allowed to seek clarifications about the system requirement. It was interesting to note that out of three bidders two did not accept the concept that the system can be fully automated. But, they continued to insist that the department should go for only stand alone electronic weigh bridges. It was the last bidder, represented by two young computer engineers looked at the concept totally differently and came out with the positive note that the system requirement proposed by the department can be implemented.

However, all the three bids were opened for further analysis and scrutiny. Two bids quoted only for electronic weigh bridges and annexed computer and peripherals. Only one bidder quoted for total solution including mechanical devices, hardware, software, installation, implementation, training, operation and maintenance for one year etc. In spite of the complete coverage of the concept, the bidder was lowest on price!

Given the limited incomparable and part proposals, the committee met and deliberated the price bids and decided to call all the three bidders once again for detailed technical presentation in the presence of technical experts from NIC, IIM, Ahmedabad and INDEXT-B. The bidders were given two hours each. Two bidders repeatedly insisted that it is advisable to go only for electronic weigh bridges without having any automation. The committee noted that the concept of complete automation of the check-posts was meant primarily to check 100 percent of the vehicles entering or exiting the state border. This checking should not only cover the load carried by the transport vehicles but also the details about the history of the vehicle and tax. This left with only one bidder who took lot of pain to study the automation available in the world and made a comprehensive automation system. On account of the detailed study carried out by this bidder and the interest shown by them in project implementation than commercial interest, the committee recommended awarding the work to this bidder, M/s Design Solutions (P) Ltd.

Cost negotiations

Though the implementing agency was identified, the task of listing out the system configuration and the technical specification for the mechanical automation devices was not detailed out. However, two young engineers, who were also the directors of the company, shown extraordinary courage in implementing the project by accepting to lower down the value to match exactly with the market prices of brand items and accept no additional leverage for profit. It appears their main aim was to make a brand name for them by successfully implementing the project and replicate elsewhere. Therefore, for 58 electronic weigh bridges and full system automation of all 58 lanes distributed in the radius of 300-400 km from the state capital, they accepted a project cost of Rs. 18.52 crore as final price. During the negotiation, it was agreed that they would install the latest version of PCs and servers from IBM, routers from CISCO, video from Philips, electronic weigh bridges from Global Weighing Ltd. (group company of General Electronic, USA) having headquarters and manufacturing base at Hamburg, Germany, and related other automation devices from the best quality available in the world.

Immediately after the negotiation, work orders were issued to the implementing agency, M/s Design Solutions (P) Ltd. The work order was very comprehensive asking for complete computerized automation of all 10 inter-state border check-posts and elimination of all manual activities at the check-posts. This gave a room to keep extending the scope of activities, which could bring many new innovations during the implementation period.

System specification

While it was decided not to compromise with the quality specification, flexibility was adapted to accommodate the suggestion and the field requirements. For example, the size of the display board for the drivers to see details of the allowed weight and actual weight was originally planned to be a huge plasma display panel similar to that of advertisement panel on top of the control cabin constructed in between two lanes but was later changed to a window size digital weight and payment indicator. Similar exercises carried out for every activity helped to arrive at the main features of the system. They are as listed below:

- All 10 inter-state border check-posts will have multiple lane operations.
- Separate lanes for traffic entering and exiting the state border.
- Each lane will have an electronic weigh bridge integrated with licence plate recognition system with online transaction process through LAN and WAN.
- Adequate lighting for night-time operations etc.
- All operations shall be automatic including the opening and closure of the barrier once the transaction is completed.
- Real time indication at headquarters.
- Online monitoring of all the check-posts from the headquarters.
- Facility to able and disable the lane operations of any check-post directly from the headquarters.
- Store the data including the photographic details of the vehicles.
- Create WAN (Wide Area Network) and LAN (Local Area Network) connectivity for online updating of data from the check-posts to headquarters.
- Establish a Central Monitoring Centre at the headquarters to monitor all 58 lanes of 10 inter-state border check-posts of the state round the clock.

Figure 3.2
Key components of the automated check-post

- Provide information access to other government departments.

The above features of the system took final shape only at the time of completion of the check-posts. With that kind of flexibility, finding an implementing agency to keep accepting the modifications till last minute and provide additional mechanization which has high additional costs was a mere luck. The implementing agency deserves full credit for constructing control cabins and huge two-floor new building of Central Monitoring Centre, which were not included in the scope of the work when the work orders were issued by the government. The final features were below:

- Primarily, the total operations were designed to clear one vehicle in two minutes, so as a single lane can clear more than 30 vehicles per hour. After the project implementation, it was a pleasant surprise to see that one vehicle clearance took only 36 seconds.
- Each lane is equipped with an electronic weigh bridge integrated with a licence plate recognition system with a video camera focused to decipher the licence plate number and send to the LAN server, which will retrieve the details of ownership of the vehicle, authorized weight, pending tax and pending judicial cases etc.
- The cabin operator would easily see full details on the computer screen but the display board kept on the window of the control cabin for the driver would display only the authorized weight of the vehicle, actual load and the payment to be paid, including tax arrears and overload penalty. These transactions can be seen and monitored in the Central Monitoring Centre located at the headquarters (RTO, Ahmedabad).
- In case the LAN system could not find the relevant information of a particular vehicle, the system is designed to automatically contact the central server at the headquarters to retrieve the details of the vehicle instantly. All the check-posts are connected through 64 kbps leased lines from the Telecom Department. In case the required information is not available in the database, the cabin operator would fill a data format to make new data entry. This would form the part of database management system henceforth. Moreover, the check-post inspector enters these formats only after the concerned RTO authenticates him.
- Once the transaction is completed, the cabin operator would collect the payments from the driver and would give clearance for the barrier to open for the vehicle to enter or

Figure 3.3

Functioning of the check-posts

Before

After

Separate lanes for different capacity vehicles

Vehicles to move on to weighbridge with turning of traffic signal from red to green

The overload and leviable fees are displayed outside the cabin on large electronic display board for the drivers to see and pay the fees

Box 3.1

Technical features

- The 10 inter-state RTO check-posts have 58 lanes and each check-post is equipped with LAN and connected with WAN system based on 64 kbps leased lines from Department of Telecom. Through this communication system all the 58 lanes are connected with DBMS and monitored through video display at the central computer-monitoring centre at Ahmedabad.
- The weigh bridge platforms are pit less and the size is 18 m x 3 m. The dead weight of each platform is 15 tonnes. Each platform can handle a vehicle up to 100 tonnes.
- Load cells and six constrainers are provided on each platform.
- The cables from load cell are connected to the amplifier and load cell processing unit located in control room.
- The printers are connected to weigh bridge terminal for printing vehicle number, dead laden weight, allowable weight, differential weight, date, time, charges for excess weight, etc.
- The server stores all data and this data is transmitted online to headquarters through a modem.
- A large display system is located in front of each weigh bridge.
- An Automatic Teller Machine (ATM) for pre-paid card insertion and gate operation is planned for cashless transaction.*
- A video camera is installed in front of weigh bridge. The camera is housed in a weather protection cover. The signal from camera is transmitted to a transmitter and further transmitted to headquarters through modem.
- The signal received through modem at headquarters is sent to a PC, which monitors display signals from more than one camera simultaneously.
- A motorized vehicle barrier and traffic signal is located in front of each weighbridge. Normally, barrier remains closed. As soon as a transaction is completed, by computerized signal the barrier opens. At the time of opening of the barrier, traffic signal will turn to 'green' from 'red'.
- Auto/manual gate opening system through ATM is also planned.
- Computer, modem and printer are located in control room.
- The entire system is provided with UPS for one hour.
- A back-up generator shall start in case of prolonged power failure.

* It couldn't be implemented because of RBI norms.

exit the border. The sensor located near the barrier automatically closes the barrier once the vehicle has crossed.

- Originally, the payment transactions were designed through a pre-paid smart card operation system. Since the outlet for the pre-paid smart card to be issued had to be created at every check-post, the Reserve Bank of India (RBI) took objections stating that the norms to treat these outlets as a branch of a bank. Because of this condition only Centurion Bank came forward to issue the pre-paid smart cards. But, after two months, they also withdrew because of operational inconveniences and non-compliance of RBI norms by declaring every check-post outlet as a bank branch. Therefore, the cash payment system continued at the check-posts.
- Once the payment transaction is completed, the computer signal opens the barrier for the vehicle to proceed. To replace the cash payment pre-paid, a smart card also is being planned, which is expected to be in place in another twelve months.
- On completion of every transaction and once the vehicle move out of the platform, the sensor placed parallel to the video camera closes the barrier and sends signal from 'red' to 'green' for the next vehicle to move in.
- Time taken for this transaction is about two minutes.

Advancement of computerized automation

Once the lane system is defined, artificial intelligence was planned to equip the mechanical devices. Conceptually easy for a video camera to read a licence plate was the toughest task because of the varieties of Indian style of writing of numbers in the licence plate. A total of 72 different styles and letters were written in vernacular languages like Hindi, Gujarati etc. A team consisting of video camera experts (Philips India Ltd.), electronic weigh bridge experts (Global Weighing), computer hardware engineers, computer software engineers, a small group of RTO inspectors and a system integrator worked 24 hours during the monsoon for a period of one month to develop the licence plate recognition system. Dusty roads, mud sling and partly twisted number plates were the tremendous problems for a video camera to use its intelligence to convert the display image to correct registration number of the transport vehicle. It was a daunting task and the great challenge was to evolve an error-free artificial intelligence system. But, the team did not compromise at all even for 0.001 percent error. This team effort brought accuracy to the licence plate recognition system and it became the first system to have artificial intelligence in an e-governance project in India.

With this major breakthrough, aligning the mechanical devices was very easy but time-consuming. The next task was to create the network connectivity to the check-posts located at the remote places of the state. The General Manager, Telecom Department, Ahmedabad was approached to provide 64 kbps connectivity to all the check-posts on leased line basis. Since the Transport Department, Government of Gujarat was the first government agency to ask for such leased line connectivity that too for remote places, the Telecom Department found it very difficult to get approval from their head office at New Delhi. After having a meeting with a member of the Telecom Board at New Delhi, it expedited the whole process and the local telephone exchanges were permitted to procure Max Card to install in their exchanges located near the check-posts. Normally, data transmission would be slow if aluminium conductors are used and therefore the Telecom Department was requested to lay optical fibre from the exchange to the check-posts, which they readily agreed at a fee. When there are 12 lanes in a check-post, 64 kbps leased line cannot be expected to transfer graphic details speedily and hence it warranted to build flexibility to dilute the graphic resolution so as even during peak hours also the digital data with diluted graphic picture frames reach headquarters speedily.

Salient features of the automation

This project is not only unique in Asia but also in the world because of its graphic data storage and graphic monitoring. The

Figure 3.4

Computerised licence plate recognition system

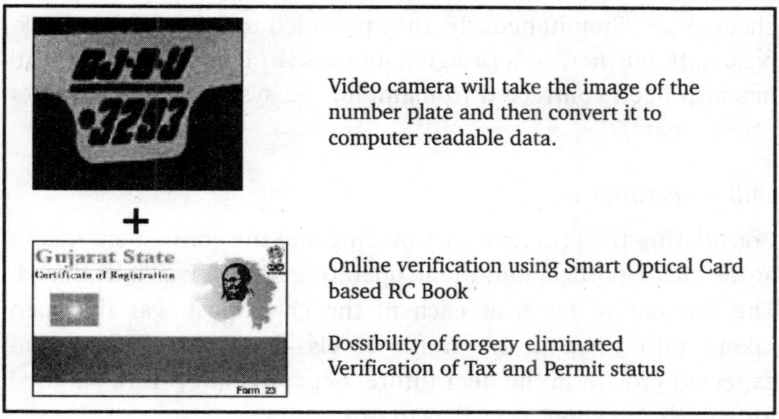

Ministry of Transport, Canada and the California Transport System (USA) use the graphic database system to monitor traffic flow and also the highway 407 from Toronto to Baffalo uses LPR for toll collection. Keeping this concept in mind the inter-state check-posts project is designed to suit the Indian system where 80 percent of the traffic is of commercial vehicles and most of them carry oversize and overload.

The video placed in each lane not only functions as LPR but also sends data to the Central Monitoring Centre located at Ahmedabad. This computerized monitoring centre would have online display of every lane of all the 10 inter-state check-posts and operators round the clock would monitor the vehicles movement of every six lanes. The supervisor from the centre can disable the check-post operation and can directly operate the whole or part of the check-post. This enables flexibility and effective control. The entry and exit of every vehicle's data is stored for a period of six months in the database in graphic and this would be useful in case if any vehicle owner wants to trace their vehicle movement. The 64 kbps leased line communication network is planned to be strengthened in case of increased future need.

M/s Design Solutions (P) Limited, Ahmedabad implemented the project operated all the check-posts for a period of 12 months immediately after the installation and commissioning of the check-posts. Simultaneously, they provided training to the check-post staff. Further, M/s Design Solutions (P) Limited, Ahmedabad has also been contracted to maintain the system for a period of fifteen years.

Online operations

Considering the problems of crowding and the consequent delays at the check-posts, a multi-lane operating system was introduced. The number of lanes at each of the check-post was designed taking into account the traffic levels—both the present and expected growth in the near future. Separate lanes were planned for vehicles to enter as well as to exit.

Separate lanes were kept for vehicles of different carrying capacity. Any vehicle crossing the border first enters either in the lane for more than 100 tonnes or into the lane of less than 100 tonnes. Light motor vehicles and non-tax levied vehicles cross the check-post through the speed lanes marked with only height barrier in between the outgoing and incoming lanes. While, on the lane, once the traffic signal turns from 'red' to 'green', the vehicle moves on to the weigh bridge platform and stops parallel to the large electronic display board kept on the cabin. At this stage, the traffic signal turns from 'green' to 'red'. The video camera, positioned to read the number plate, reads and sends the graphic data and digital data to headquarters and retrieves the ownership, tax details to display on the VDU in front of the operator sitting in the cabin. Simultaneously, the permissible load and the overload if any with leviable fees are displayed in the large electronic display. Once the payment transaction is completed, the computer signal opens the barrier for the vehicle to proceed. As stated earlier, to replace the cash payment, a pre-paid smart card is also planned, which is expected to be in place soon.

Figure 3.5

Central monitoring office

(a) Online monitoring of all ten inter-state border check-posts

(b) Check-post transactions: viewed at the central monitoring office

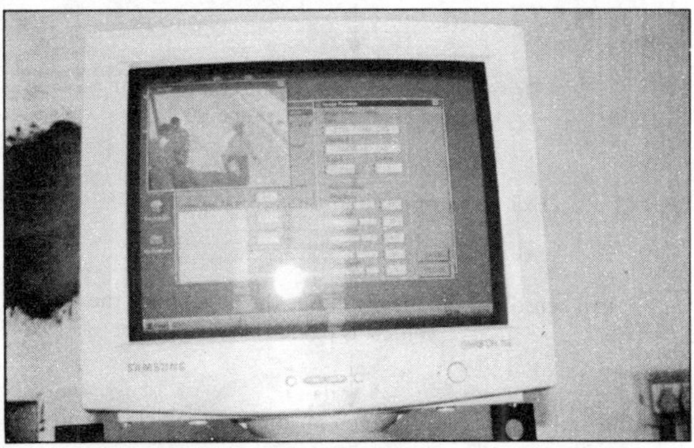

Figure 3.6

Check-post clearance procedure

Transport vehicles arrive for entry and exit

↓

Inter-state border RTO check-post of Gujarat

↓

Align the vehicles in lanes

↓

Enters into electronic weigh bridge lane on green traffic signal

↓

Video camera reads the vehicle number and sends it to the lane scanner

↓

Licence plate requisition system downloads ownership and tax details of the vehicle

↓

Display panel displays the tax arrears, load currently carried, load permissible, penalty if any and total payment to be made

↓

Driver pays at the lane counter and system gives the clearance

↓

Exit panel opens and the vehicle exits

↓

Exit sensor automatically closes the panel once the vehicle is passed

↓

Traffic red signal turns to green for the next vehicle to enter

On completion of every transaction and once the vehicle moves out of the platform the sensor placed parallel to the video camera closes the barrier and sends signal from 'red' to 'green' for the next vehicle to move in. Time taken for this transaction is about two minutes.

Hurdles faced

A series of hurdles, technical as well as administrative, were faced by the project during implementation. Through collaborative support from other departments of the government, openness of the vendor and active involvement from the employees, the hurdles were successfully overcome and implementation was done in eight months against the planned period of twelve months. Two problems were critical and have been described in more details below:

Land acquisition

The first problem faced was the land acquisition in remote places and that belonged to *Adivasis*. Legally, their lands cannot be acquired unless their consent and a special permission are obtained from the government. The project was planned for completion within 12 months. Land acquisition itself was expected to take more than one year. There was a necessity to find a way to close the acquisition process within 60 days and commence construction activities of concrete bridges at the height of 25 metres with a breadth of 125 metres and roads etc. The Roads & Buildings Department was found extremely efficient in coordinating with their field offices in all 10 check-posts. Continuous meetings with the affected landholders and accepting to their estimated cost and a promise to compensate them with allotment of equal land nearby made it possible to complete the land acquisition proceedings in a record time of 90 days. Being open minded, continued communication, listening to their side of the story and accepting their reasoning made this possible.

Technical difficulties

Once the possession of the land was taken over by the Roads & Buildings Department, they immediately commenced the road laying activities, which included cutting number of hillocks and constructing number of concrete bridges at the height of 25 metres and breadth of 125 metres and culverts etc. While the Roads & Buildings Department were at it, our implementing agency was finding it very difficult to design appropriate foundations for the electronic weight bridges. In addition, monsoon further delayed the implementation process. Since the implementing agency had its core strength of only computer engineers, it hired outside agency for civil works. After a period of four months, it realized that the foundations designed were faulty and the construction activities could not commence. A public sector undertaking (National Building Construction Corporation—NBCC) was then requested to undertake these works, which they readily agreed. In spite of this, it was not profitable to them as NBCC got the designs from IIT, Mumbai, requiring special structural expertise to calculate the stress on the structure when the vehicles move with a load of 50-100 MTs. Once the structural design was ready, NBCC moved very fast and completed the foundation work, cabins of the check-posts, monitoring centres at the check-posts and Central Monitoring Centre at Ahmedabad in a record time of four months. Thus, the speed of work carried out by Roads & Buildings Department and NBCC was the key element to complete the project within 10 months.

Innovative projects often run into technical problems, which may incur additional costs. When we introduced licence plate recognition system, we planned number plate vending machine to issue uniform number plates for easy reading by the video camera. But, the issue was who would do it and how to cover the cost. In addition to operational uncertainty problems, legality on procurement aspects also came in between and as a result it could not be implemented. Further, the Central Monitoring Centre was not covered in the project scope, as it was not conceived at the initial stage. And, there was no funding provision from the approved budget. It was extremely good on the part of the implementing agency that they agreed to construct at their cost in the interest of the project. Such additional contingencies to absorb such costs need to be incorporated into the project estimate which is normally not possible in the government system.

Commencement of operations

The work orders were issued in the third week of June 1999 and the first check-post was inaugurated on 1st March 2000 by the Chief Minister of Gujarat at Bhilad near Vapi on Mumbai-Ahmedabad National Highway. This is the busiest RTO check-post in the country because it is situated on the trunk route of Mumbai-Delhi. At the time of inauguration, the Chief Minister mentioned that he was astonished to see the layout of the 12 lanes at the length of 2.5 km and appreciated the officers who thought of it, planned and implemented. Further, he said that he is thrilled to see that how the concept was conceived. With this kind of inauguration of the first fully computerized automation of the RTO check-post, the Chief Minister called the team to complete all check-posts immediately so that all the check-posts could be made operational in a row with 15 days' gap. On his call the team accepted the challenging task and completed all check-posts by August 2000.

Again, some efforts to raise issue about procurement process were made by vested interest groups. The vendors, who did not get the work order, were motivated by a few handful and raised questions about the cost, procurement procedures etc. It is remarkable to note that the first 60 days' revenue collection from only one check-post from March 1st to March 15th saw the full recovery of the cost of all 10 check-posts, i.e., Rs. 18.5 crores. Once the other check-posts started one by one, the word of mouth marketing started spreading and brought popularity of this project from all parts of the world. With this all issues got cleared automatically.

Figure 3.7

Times of India, September 6, 2000

Gujarat charts new course in e-governance

By Bharat Desai

AHMEDABAD: It's a miracle of sorts. A prime example of how e-governance can transform a wing of the government that was once plagued by corruption and red tape. And this is happening in Gujarat — not Chandrababu Naidu's Andhra or S M Krishna's Karnataka!

When some of Naidu's men came snooping last month on the state's elaborate computerised system of border check-posts, the officials of the transport department knew that recognition for the exercise had come. In what is seen as the first real execution of e-governance in the country, all 10 entry points by road to the state now have an integrated computerised system for collecting revenue and identifying offenders fool-proof.

The results have been stupendous. In the last six months, the number of commercial vehicles passing through Gujarat has come down by 30 per cent for fear of being booked for evasion. But if you think that's cause of worry for the state government, you are mistaken. The daily earnings of the check-posts has grown more than three folds — from an average of Rs 10-12 lakh per day to the present Rs 35-40 lakh per day.

How has this happened? Ask transport commissioner P Panneervel, the man who was entrusted with this elaborate licence plate recognition (LPR) system. The system was modelled along the lines of the LPR between Toronto and Niagara, complete with a centralised computerised monitoring centre.

Panneervel says, "Everyone knows that this department was known to be one of the most corrupt. We thought, instead of suspending inspectors and clerks for corruption, how if we could correct the system." The LPR system cost the government Rs 18.51 crore which would be recovered in six months time.

TRANSPORT DEPT REVENUE

YEAR	FROM CHECK POSTS	TOTAL
1997-98......	Rs 36 cr	Rs 432 cr
1998-99......	Rs 55 cr	Rs 510 cr
1999-00......	Rs 93 cr	Rs 686 cr
2000-01...... *(estimated)*	Rs 250 cr	—

"It's very simple. Our system scans the registration plates of the vehicle and all the details appear on the screen, including the weight of the load and the tax dues." Trucks cannot pass the check-post without clearing all dues. The element of corruption is eliminated as all 58 lanes at the check-posts are monitored on 58 video screens in the central control room in Ahmedabad.

"Earlier, we used to check only 2 per cent vehicles. Now we can do that to all vehicles," says Panneervel. As a result, he says, a lot of tax evaders, transporters who overload their vehicles or those who do not have valid papers skirt round Gujarat and enter Madhya Pradesh. "But we are not worried. Though the number of commercial vehicles passing through Gujarat has gone down by 30 per cent, our collections have more than tripled," he says.

The computerised check-posts have already boosted the revenue projections of the transport department for the year 2000-2001 to Rs 900 crore — up from Rs 686 crore last year. The collections from the check-posts alone will show a spectacular jump — from Rs 93 crore to Rs 250 crore in the same period.

No wonder then that Naidu sent his men to have a close look at the miracle Gujarat has just performed. And Maharashtra, Madhya Pradesh, Rajasthan , West Bengal and Orissa have also evinced keen interest as the word spreads.

THE TIMES OF INDIA, AHMEDABAD — WEDNESDAY, SEPTEMBER 6, 2000

MIS maintenance

The main server located at the head office in Ahmedabad has a parallel server in the same station and is designed to have a duplicate server in Gandhinagar in case of any fire, accident, etc. As of now, the communication network is connected by 64 kbps DoT leased line from the Ahmedabad head office to all the check-posts, RTO offices and ARTO offices. Out of three MIS applications, the main applications of registration of vehicles, income account, driving licence have been completed and installed. A database is also being created for the commercial vehicles. On completion of the installations of software for all the thirteen applications, the functions of the Transport Department would be integrated. However, software related to the check-posts operations are fully installed and connected with the communication network of DoT leased lines from the head office to the check-posts.

The result

The result of the project would have to be seen in terms of the revenue potential realized and convenience provided to the customers.

Realization of revenue potential

As stated earlier, the Transport Department is one of the major revenue-earning departments in the state. During 1996-97 and 1997-98 annual revenue earnings were in the range of Rs. 4,300 million. Because of recession, during 1998-99, the estimated revenue was Rs. 3,500 million only. This was a matter of concern, however, the steps taken to arrest the corrupt practices of the field staff and increased percentage of vehicle checking could yield revenue collection upto Rs. 5,096 million. But, these measures were temporary and, therefore, it was proposed to have a permanent and long-term solution to have sustainable higher revenue. It was thought that this can be achieved only by increased percentage of checking from prevailing 2 percent to 100 percent and evolve a system to arrest corrupt practices totally. Therefore, it was decided to implement fully automated and computerized inter-state border check-posts which can be centrally monitored. This project was designed to be world class with state-of-the-art technology. It was expected to double the revenue, but it increased manifold. Keeping high revenue earning potential in mind, the government approved the project at a total cost of Rs. 180 million.

The graph illustrated in Figure 3.8 clearly shows that the state-of-the-art technology put to use to streamline the procedures enhanced the revenue from Rs. 310 million in 1997-98 to Rs. 2908.3 million in 2003-04, which could go up to Rs. 1,665 million in 2000-01, which is almost 9 times higher. Information technology applications implemented resulted in this increase in revenue. Further, the introduction of the e-governance concept in the inter-state border check-posts increased not only their income manifold, but also could provide valuable information to the field offices, which further used it as a tool to enhance their revenue.

Figure 3.8

Increased revenues of check-posts

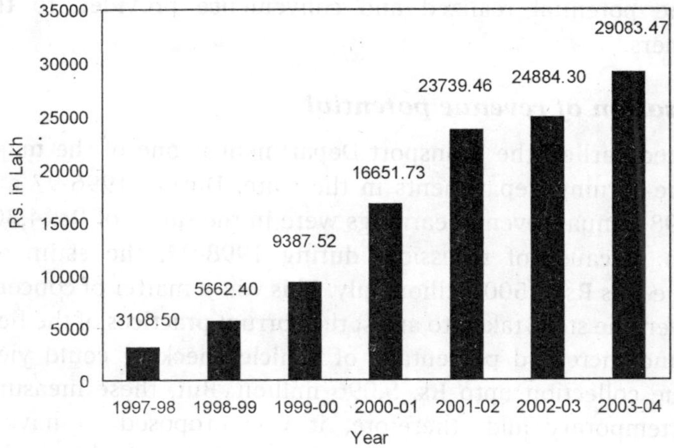

Benefits to the customers

The transporters also expressed their experience as that of user-friendly and transparent. Further, it does not provide any room for malpractices from transporters' employees or from the government employees. The system also enables them to watch the movement of the vehicles crossing the inter-state border. Compared to long waiting period to cross-check the paper-based information from the field offices, now, the online information totally eliminates the waiting period. This user-friendly system has totally removed the harassment meted out to the transporters. The Gujarat Transport Association expressed its appreciation that this user-friendly state-of-the-art technology based, inter-state border check-posts should be implemented in all other states also.

More specifically, the significant benefits to the consumers are:

- The clearance time for the vehicles has been reduced drastically. Hence, harassment has been eliminated.
- Uncertainty of location due to unlimited detention of their vehicles at the check-posts was a major fear factor for

Table 3.1

Income of check-posts from 1997-98 to 2004-05

(Rs. in lakh)

Sr. No.	*Name of office*	*1997-98*	*1998-99*	*1999-02*	*2000-01*	*2001-02*	*2002-03*	*2003-04*
1	Bhilad	941.01	1591.72	2636.49	3925.73	5088.16	5073.80	5728.77
2	Shamlaji	641.39	1228.94	1926.46	3379.14	4611.68	4713.50	4988.41
3	Songadh	309.00	687.22	1224.84	2286.12	3580.93	3986.22	4660.47
4	Amirgadh	335.31	705.40	1253.80	2345.00	3045.74	2353.63	2607.16
5	Deesa	262.22	652.97	1068.95	1659.00	2087.48	2846.54	2785.30
6	Dahod	248.23	318.17	572.16	905.99	1100.47	1119.23	1423.92
7	Zalod	40.11	56.03	110.62	128.04	143.77	151.29	197.62
8	Tharad	56.58	165.86	345.81	435.42	654.66	851.70	1275.15
9	Ambaji	222.93	198.70	170.81	196.15	212.45	235.09	256.95
10	Samakhiyali	0.00	0.00	0.00	1307.44	3108.49	2787.65	3801.30
11	Waghai	51.72	57.39	77.58	83.70	105.63	129.34	158.92
12	Jamnagar						636.31	1058.70
13	Chhota Udepur							140.80
14	Bhavnagar Alang							351.27
	Total	3108.50	5662.40	9387.52	16651.70	23739.50	24884.30	29083.50

Source: Commissioner of Transport, Government of Gujarat.

transport companies. This has now been removed. Now, the operator can be certain about the entry and exit timing of the vehicle within the state.

- Transparent transaction enables the customer to claim tax exemptions for the amount paid.
- Due to reduction in corruption, the cost of transport would have reduced significantly.

Conclusion

The success of the project was visible immediately. Though, it took some time to clear the initial teething problems, the visible results ensured that the project is in full operation. Designing of the system in-house to suit various activities was the key success factor. The project received wide publicity. The World Bank published two case studies—one in the beginning and next after two years of operation. These studies also included recommendations for further improvement and replication. Despite the results being visible and the benefits reaped by the state in the form of increased revenue, till date (October 2004) there is no information available about replication in any other states. The Information Technology Department of the Government of India, in its report for the year 2003-04, listed Gujarat as a leader in e-governance because of its projects like computerized automation of RTO check-posts, smart card driving licence system and smart optical card-based registration book for vehicles etc.

4

Optical Card Registration Certificate Book

Introduction of Optical Card Registration Certificate (RC) Book was a logical extension of the e-governance initiatives carried out by the Transport Department during the period from 1998 to 2000. The two successful applications initiated early include a smart card-based driving licence with biometric identification and full computerization of all inter-state border RTO check-posts. Once these were covered under the e-governance system, major areas left out were the Registration Certificate (RC) book and related Management Information System (MIS). For RC book application, it was preferred to go for smart card device similar to that of the driving licence but the difference here was the large amount of information that required to be recorded. This was designed after a series of consultations with stakeholders.

As per the provision in sections 42, 43 and 60 of the Motor Vehicles Act, 1988, every owner of a motor vehicle has to make the registration of the vehicle under the authority in whose jurisdiction it falls. Further, the owner is expected to carry RC book as the legal identity card of the vehicle.

The RC book gives details about ownership of the vehicle, its registration number, technical details of the vehicle, amount of load it is allowed to carry, payment of vehicle tax, fitness status, etc. Any change in the address, transfer of ownership, hypothecation agreement, termination of hypothecation agreement, alteration in the vehicle, etc. should be informed to the Registering Authority.

As per the Motor Vehicles Act, 1988, registration of any vehicle has been made in line with the tax payment requirement. Registration for personal vehicles is done at the time of purchase and the tax paid is also valid for 15 years (lifetime tax). Whereas in case of commercial vehicles[1] it is essential to have a fitness certificate without which the registration is invalid. Again, the fitness certificate has to be renewed every year; hence, they have to renew the registration every year. The vehicle is inspected before renewal of registration. The owner of the commercial vehicle has to pay the tax every year or half-yearly or quarterly. Details of payment of tax are entered in the RC book and updated regularly.

Thus, the main purposes served by the RC book are:

- Identity of the vehicle through a unique registration number given by RTO.
- Fitness check through Vehicle Fitness Certificate.
- Record keeping of tax payment.

Problems of paper RC book

The paper-based RC book has several associated problems. Major amongst them are:

- *Condition of the book:* The RC book is repeatedly used. Because of frequent handling and exposure to bad weather conditions, the lifetime of the paper RC book is reduced to one or two years.
- *Forgery/fake certificate:* The book is easy to copy, forge or fake.
- *Limited scope for verification:* Commercial vehicles have to get the permit to use the vehicle either within the state or in

1. 'Transport or commercial vehicle' means any motor vehicle used for carrying passengers or goods or both by road for hire or reward. Buses, trucks, vans, tourist taxis, auto-rickshaws, staff vehicle of private companies, tempos, jeeps are all classified as transport/commercial vehicles.

other states (national permit). Once in a year a team of senior officers visits other states to clear and cross-check some copies of national permits. However, the scale of verification is so small that it becomes impossible to verify.

- *Operational problems:* Due to ledger-based tax maintenance and ineffective links between RTO offices, there is no reconciliation for non-payment of tax. The official records are poorly maintained and stored in an area accessible to general public, thus gets damaged very fast. Search of old records on many occasions is impossible, especially if the vehicle is transferred to or sold in other districts.
- *Growth of vehicle population:* Recent spurt of automobile vehicle growth (Table 4.1) increased the paper works manifolds, particularly when there was no proportionate growth of manpower to maintain and manage such records. Transporters found it convenient to fake the records and documents of commercial transport vehicles to evade tax.

Table 4.1

Growth of vehicle population

Year	*Number of vehicles*	*Growth percentage*
1998-99	4679793	11%
1999-2000	5190732	11%
2000-01	5576040	7%
2001-02	6007969	8%
2002-03	6508370	8%
2003-04	7087490	9%

Source: Commissioner of Transport, Government of Gujarat, 2004.

These result into:

- *Evasion of taxes:* Forged or fake certificates, which means loss of revenue in the form of taxes, fee and charges.

- *Scope for financial frauds:* It is also common to see use of fake certificates to avail multiple bank loans.

The Transport Department found out an interesting case of misuse, where 11 buses carried one registration number but having 11 RC books of same registration number. It was physically impossible to catch all the 11 buses at a time and prove the tax evasion. The bus owners pay tax for only one bus and use the copies of the RC book for the rest of 11 buses having the same number. The annual taxes for the buses are high and range from Rs. 2,500 to Rs. 7,000 per seat. Many bus operators find the tax very high and their business becomes economically unviable. Because of this reason, forgery of RC books and evasion of taxes are common with the connivance of the employees of the RTO offices where the vehicles are registered. As per the general estimate, 30 to 50 percent of the tax is not collected due to inadequate supervision of tax assessment.[2]

Similar cases of forgery were found in case of goods vehicles also. Generally, the owners forge RC books by making entry of higher tonnage carrying capacity so as to become eligible to carry more load than the legally authorized load. Lifetime tax on vehicles varies with size and load carrying capacity of the vehicles. Hence, the order of tax evasion ascends in the same pattern. Grading of tax evasion ascends from medium size transport vehicle (8 to 10 MTs), commercial transport vehicles (12 to 18 MTs), heavy transport vehicles (20 to 30 MTs) to the passenger buses and the luxury coaches. In the lure of permanent tax evasion, there are also cases where heavy transport vehicles are sold and transferred to other districts, but with the connivance of RTO office employees the communication is sent as auto-rickshaws (three-wheelers).

The competitiveness among the transport industry constantly forces cost cutting measures, whereas the ever-increasing fuel prices necessitate adjustments where possible. Moreover, there is large difference in the tax amount between state-owned bus and the private sector bus transport system. For example, the Gujarat

2. Refer Annexure-I

State Road Transport Corporation pays 17 percent of the passenger tax from their total annual income whereas the private operators have to pay anywhere between Rs. 2,500 and Rs. 7,500 per seat per annum, irrespective of the seat occupancy rate. This means an investment of Rs. 10 lakh to procure a bus demands annual tax of Rs. 2 lakh to 5 lakh. The bus operators found tax rates very difficult to comply with and put efforts to evade them by all means.

Solution

Because of such huge tax evasion, the Transport Department sought a foolproof solution leveraging IT tools:

- User-friendly
- Fully secured
- Tamper-proof
- Durable and with a possibility to upgrade in future
- Seamlessly integrated with other IT applications of the department
- Provides effective tax collection mechanism
- Provides effective enforcement off-line checking mechanism on road

The smart card driving licence system concept was extended to suit the requirement. The main difference between the two is that operational data required for driving licence is small whereas the RC book needs to carry much more information including the history of the court cases. The essential information required are listed out as follow:

- Vehicle owners' details
- The class of vehicle and authorized load
- Unique identification of the vehicle
- Trails of sales and transactions
- Secured signature (electronic signature of the RC book receiving authority)
- Vehicle owners identification like signatures/thumb impression etc.

Figure 4.1

Putting it altogether in an optical card

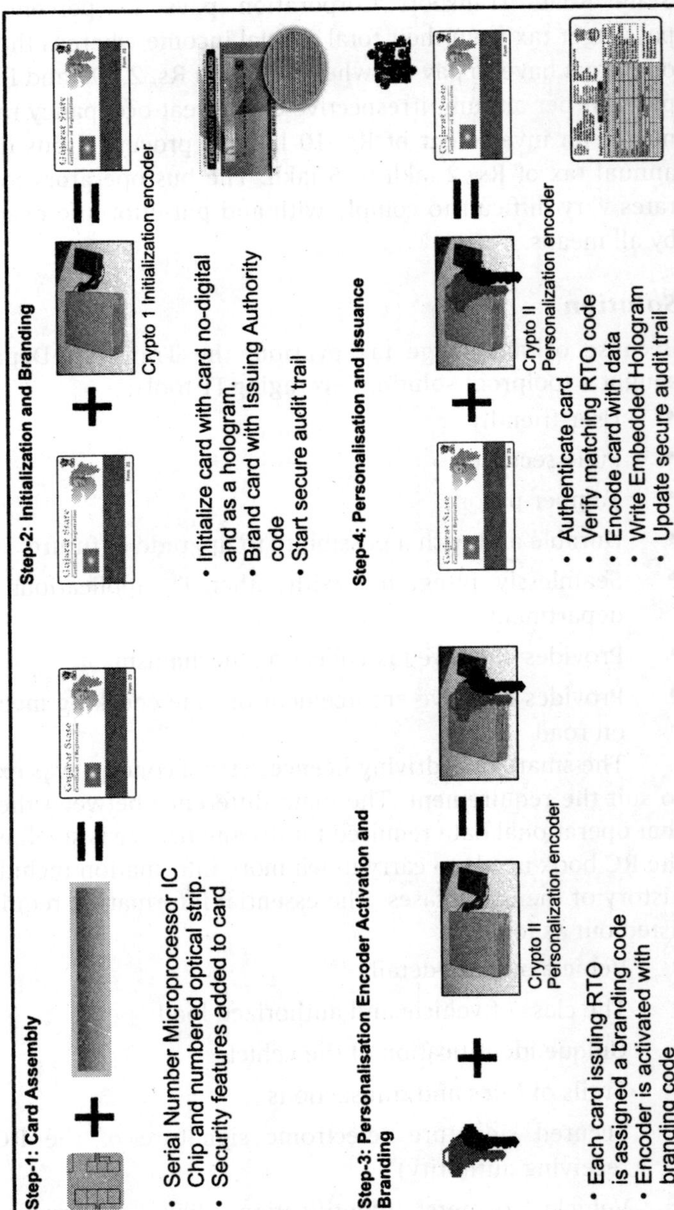

Some additional informations that were introduced in the RC book include:

- Pollution under control certificates
- Previous insurance claims
- Accident-related police cases
- Previous action cases related to tax evasion or overloading etc.

It was also important that all the above information pertaining to the vehicles are readable across the country. Considering the requirements, it was thought that a smart card having memory chip of 4 kb and an optical strip of 1.5 mb (can carry almost 1,200 pages information in A-4 size paper) should be the right solution. One of the advantages for selecting this was also that the memory chip could be fused after authorized information is recorded, whereas the lengthy case history could be recorded in the optical strip. This hybrid smart card was the first of its kind in the world. But it has limitation of its readability on the road because the memory chip readers are handheld whereas the optical readers are heavy and desktop.

The total RC book could be accommodated in a compact plastic card of size 2" x 4", plus the backside of the card was specially designed to carry the full format of the form 23A of Indian Motor Vehicles Act.

Figure 4.2
Smart optical RC book

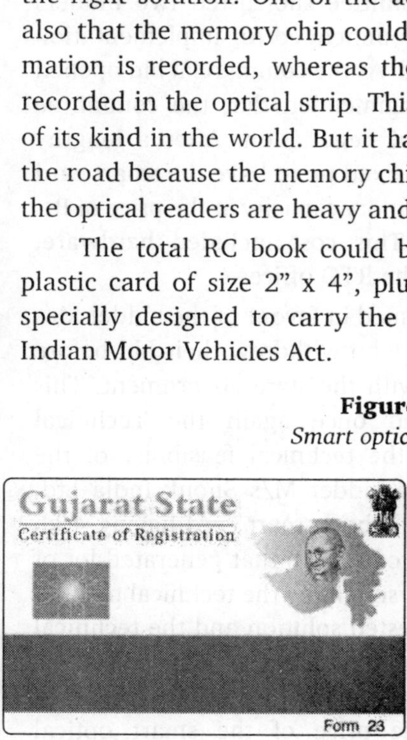

Front side view

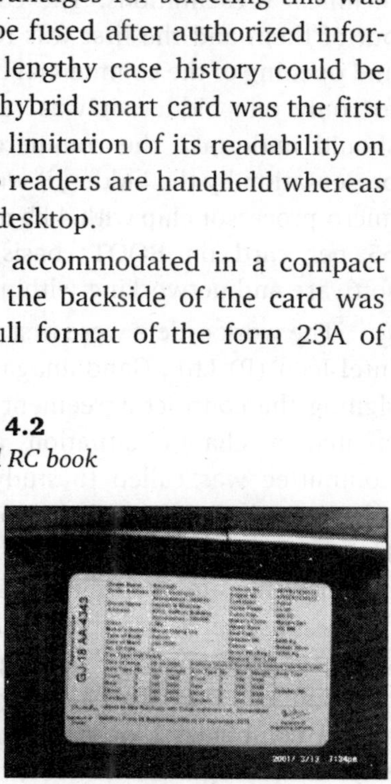

Backside view

Implementation

Tenders were called for the procurement procedures. During the first pre-bid meeting, the system requirement was explained. Then, the bidders were allowed to visit the RTO offices and study existing system in detail for a period of 30 days and submit the solution in two parts (technical bid and commercial bid). The perspective bidders further sought for another pre-bid meeting in which all their questions were answered by the Transport Commissioner and other officials.

The submitted solutions were evaluated by a committee consisting of Secretary Transport; Secretary, Information Technology; and technical experts from IIM, Ahmedabad, NIC and INDEXT-B. There were in all 21 bidders and 17 of them made technical presentations. The committee shortlisted two bidders out of them and the first was recommended for implementation and opening of the commercial bid. As the commercial bid opened for only one bidder, it was recommended that the committee should undertake the commercial negotiation. After a lengthy presentation by the bidder, it was fixed up to have the smart card micro-processor chip with 4 kb memory capacity at the price of Rs. 65 per card on BOOT[3] basis. This cost included hardware, software and networking within the RTO offices.

The work orders were first issued in favour of the bidder M/s Intel Icon (P) Ltd., Gandhinagar, who withdrew their bid before signing the contract agreement with the state government. This created a chaotic situation and once again the Technical Committee was called to study the technical feasibility of the solution submitted by the second bidder M/s Shonk India Ltd. They suggested the solution of a hybrid smart card having 4 kb memory chip and an optical strip of 1.5 mb that generated lot of discussions. Again, more time was sought by the technical team to study the workability of the suggested solution and the technical presentation was called after a gap of two weeks. This one was a hybrid combination of smart card, so security issue was deliberated at length. Therefore, the price of the smart optical

3. BOOT: Build, Own, Operate & Transfer is a type of public-private partnership.

card-based RC book was also little higher—Rs. 250 per vehicle. The Purchase Committee, after a series of meetings, concluded with the recommendation to implement the project on BOOT basis and allowed the bidder to charge Rs. 250 per RC book as administrative charges.

For all the commercial vehicles, smart optical card RC book was made mandatory whereas for non-commercial vehicle owners it was obligatory to decide between paper-based RC book or smart optical card-based RC book.

RC book enrolment process

Step 1. Application

For registration of a new vehicle, an application may be submitted in form 21 by the motor vehicle dealers.

Step 2. Data entry

After obtaining details of the name and address of the vehicle purchaser, appropriate data entry is made in the duly prescribed

Figure 4.3
RC database record

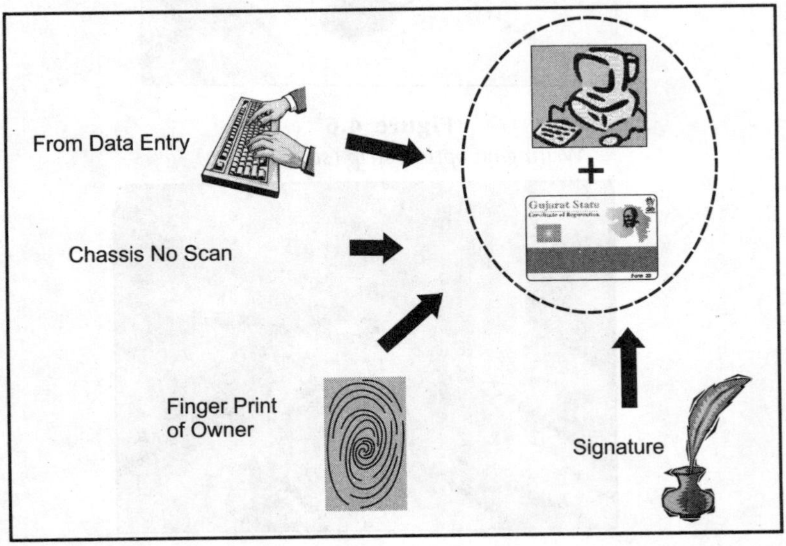

Figure 4.4
Writing on chips

Figure 4.5
Biometrics recording

Figure 4.6
Writing on optical strip (storage data)

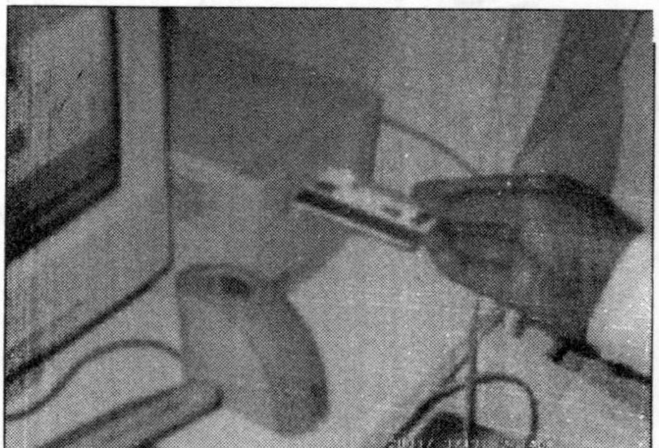

form. Simultaneously, the engine number and the chassis number are entered through a laser gun.

Step 3. Unique identity generation

The system is designed to generate its unique 10-digit PIN for identification, which would be known only to the system. This is encrypted into the memory chip of the smart card for identification etc. As a precaution, the fingerprints of the owner are also taken and stored in the system as well as in the smart card RC book.

Step 4. Clearance of registration

After the data entry is completed, the vehicle inspection is carried out by the inspector, who is authorized to clear the registration through LAN system. Fully completed formats flagged to RTO, who is the authorized officer to issue RC book.

Step 5. Fees payment and issue of RC book

Once the RTO office system verifies all pre-determined parameters and clears through the LAN system, the implementing agency takes the administrative charges of Rs. 250 from the owner and updates all data to the motor vehicle registration certificate database. These data are updated automatically in all RTO offices and in all inter-state borders RTO check-posts of the state.

Liberty taken in the contract

The Motor Vehicles Act prescribes the fees for RC book and only RTO inspectors are authorized to sign the receipt and collect the fees. Since this project was implemented on BOOT basis, it was cumbersome to get notification issued from the state government authorizing the bidder to collect the fees. To circumvent the legal lacunae, the bidder was allowed to collect Rs. 250 as administrative charges instead of fees. However, the legality of administrative charges collected by the implementing agency still remains as an issue.

Benefits

This RC book innovation was not well received by the users because the paper-based RC book is free of cost but the smart optical RC book costs Rs. 250 per card. It was extremely difficult to educate the motor vehicle owners about the advantages of the smart optical card of RC book. In spite of poor response, the RTO offices outstandingly stand to gain out of the new system in doubling the tax collection since last three years. The benefits to the owners of the vehicles and to the government are different here.

Table 4.2

Rates charged in different states for vehicle registration certificate

State	*Rate per card*	*Smart card vehicle registration certificate*
Gujarat	200/- for 2-wheeler 400/- for 4-wheeler 600/- for commercial categories of vehicles	Card having capacity of 4 kb memory chip with 1.5 mb optical storage
Maharashtra	350/-	Card with 4 kb micro-processor chip with additional 1.5 mb optical storage
Delhi	370/-	Card with 4 kb micro-processor chip with additional 1.5 mb optical storage
Uttar Pradesh	440/-	Card with 4 kb micro-processor chip with additional 1.5 mb optical storage
Madhya Pradesh	275/-	Card with 4 kb micro-processor chip only
West Bengal	350/-	Card with 4 kb micro-processor chip only

Figure 4.7

Times of India, September 7, 2000

THE TIMES OF INDIA

ember 7, 2000 Late City

Bennett, Coleman & Co., Ltd.

24 Pages including 6

'Hybrid cards' likely to leave vehicle thieves at their wits' end

Benefits to the vehicle owners

- Durable
- Convenient to carry
- Easy verification
- Less harassment by RTO/check-posts
- Updated tax records

The smart optical cards are being issued from seven RTO centres because it is optional for the vehicle owner to go either for paper-based RC book or smart optical RC book. The Government of Gujarat is considering now making it uniform for all kinds of vehicles to have smart optical card compulsory. In case it is decided, then the cards shall be issued on compulsory basis from all RTO centres across the state. Total smart optical card vehicle registration certificates issued as on 30 September, 2004 are 2,38,732.

Table 4.3

Smart optical card-based vehicle registration certificate issued in Gujarat (as on 30 September, 2004)

Centres	*Ahme-dabad*	*Vado-dara*	*Gandhi-nagar*	*Meh-sana*	*Nadiad*	*Rajkot*	*Surat*	*Total*
2-wheelers	82233	18796	26652	17434	10918	9651	43990	209674
3-wheelers	-	60	3	-	-	1	-	64
4-wheelers	5547	10610	3818	2841	585	92	4628	28121
Commercial	299	452	6	2	9	-	105	873
Total	88079	29918	30479	20277	11512	9744	48723	238732

Benefits to government

The major tax evasion in Gujarat is from the national permit operations. Since the national permits are issued from other states, there is no system which can authenticate the issue of such permits. Fake permits and demand drafts against the national permit tax used to be rampant. Physical verification is the only possibility to confirm the authenticity of these permits. For such physical verification the system does not have such a huge

Figure 4.8

Increased tax revenue

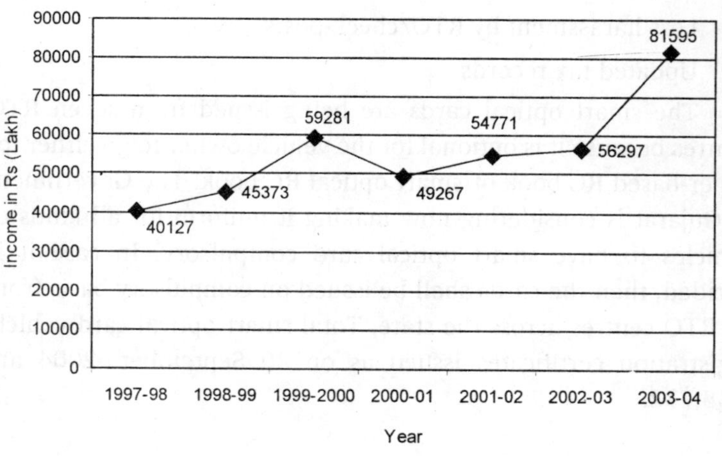

manpower to visit all RTO offices which issued national permits in the country and cross-check the records. Time and distance are the major constraints besides the requirement of huge manpower. Transporters find this inadequacy convenient to forge fake national permits to cross and operate in the states other than in those registered.

The database for this innovative hybrid card-based RC book forced a situation to create dynamic data of the particulars of the vehicles entering and exiting. Hence, continuous data creation could come out with the strong database, which could identify fake national permits over a period. Cross-verification over a period only could effectively arrest such tax evasion. On account of this database, the income of motor vehicle tax increased phenomenally.

The primary benefits of the optical card-based RC book are as follow:

- Easy identification of the tax evaders.
- Central database of all the vehicles in the state could be generated.
- It helped the department to write off most of the old tax arrears.
- Phenomenal increase in the revenue of all RTO offices.

Table 4.4

Increased tax income

(Rs. in lakh)

Name of office	*1997-98*	*1998-99*	*1999-2000*	*2000-01*	*2001-02*	*2002-03*	*2003-04*
Total (RTO/ ARTO)	31201.2	35746.1	45931.3	43000.1	42935.9	52662.6	60018.8
Total (CP)	3108.50	5662.40	9387.52	16651.7	23739.5	24884.3	29083.5
Income (CoT)	8926.2	9627.1	13349.4	6266.4	11834.8	3633.97	21576.08
Grand Total	43235.9	51035.6	68668.2	65918.3	78510.1	81180.9	110678.4

Database Management System

The ever-increasing vehicle population makes the paper-based administration impossible to collect 100 percent tax. Tax collection mechanism highly depends on the supporting data for effective monitoring. Most of the state governments, on account of economic austerity, stop filling the vacant posts even in important revenue-earning departments. This adds misery in collecting information to effectively monitor the tax defaulters. Because of high rate of tax structure, very high percentage of vehicle owners have developed tendency to evade tax. To arrest such evasion central database on tax-related information is essential. The innovation of smart optical registration card could

Figure 4.9

System architecture

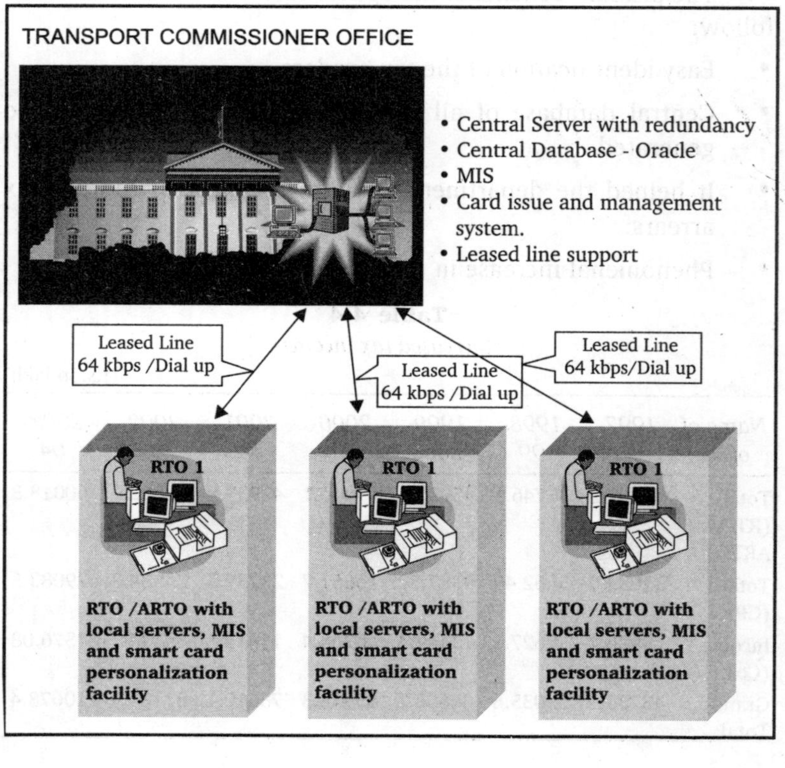

bring in a database management system (DBMS) which enable the employees to find the required information immediately, resulting in the effective monitoring of tax collection. This DBMS is integrated with other systems like inter-state border check-posts system and the general MIS.

Conclusion

This project received limited acceptance as it was not made mandatory. Benefits are perceived to accrue more to the government than to the vehicle owners. The charges fixed for the card were found to be on the higher side. Despite this, it is necessary to extend e-governance applications to such areas in order to provide total solutions. Appropriate revision in the charges of the card may perhaps make the project more acceptable.

5

Integrated Transport Management Information System

The Department of Transport deals with several functions and hence has to manage large amount of data. The nature and magnitude of data being handled has been covered to a great extent in the previous chapters. The results of manual data keeping and processing have also been explained adequately. As the e-governance application development within the department evolved incrementally over time, and major parts of the departmental functions were brought under the e-governance mechanism, integration of all of these into one unified system remained. The matter of this chapter is the final application of the Transport Department.

The Gujarat State Transport Department, having successfully completed three major projects, namely, smart card driving licence system, computerization of inter-state border RTO check-posts and smart optical card RC book, needed to bring all of them and other minor aspects under one unified system. Since all these projects were designed separately, they were functioning in parts and data aggregation and manipulation was a challenge. In order to fill up these gaps, it was decided to interlink all the systems through an Integrated Management Information System (IMIS).

The Management Information System (MIS) collects and analyzes data from all the departments and it is designed to provide up-to-date information within any organization. The computerization through MIS in Transport Department can fetch benefits like:

- Establish information linkages to capture and disseminate the data needed to support the delivery of various service.
- Easy access to data for the employees and beneficiaries.
- Improve the sophistication level of technologies in the department.
- Transparency within the department.
- Increased administrative efficiency and reduced duplicity in work.
- Lay the groundwork for increased or continued integration in the future.

The proposal was sent to the government seeking approval to implement this project as a separate one. After the due approval of the state government, a tender was released inviting bidders. A specific condition was given that the bidders should be familiar with Gujarati language and software would be developed both in English and Gujarati languages since all government employees are familiar with official correspondence in Gujarati language. Because of the strict norms stipulated, only Gujarat-based software companies participated in the bidding. A pre-bid meeting was held to clarify all queries of perspective bidders and they were asked to study the functioning of the RTO offices and Transport Commissioner office with a view that the MIS can be designed to be user-friendly. It was explained that more weightage will be given to those companies, which already have adequate experience in developing software for state government offices.

Activities required MIS

Following are the activities under various heads that require MIS:

Motor vehicle tax

- Tax collection of new vehicles
- Annual tax collection of registered transport commercial vehicles
- Bombay motor vehicle composite tax refund
- Refund of passenger tax
- Refund of fees collected under Indian Motor Vehicles Rules
- Tax on national permit

Motor vehicle registration-related activities

- Certificate of temporary registration
- Issue of trade certificate
- Registration of motor vehicles through dealer and other than dealer also
- Renewal of certificate of registration of motor vehicle
- Issue of duplicate registration certificate
- No objection certificate for vehicle transfer
- No dues certificate for vehicle transfer
- Transfer of ownership
- Change of address
- Hire purchase agreement endorsement and its termination
- Renewal of fitness certificate

Issue of permits at head office

- All-India tourist permit issue and authorization of tourist permit
- Renewal of tourist permit
- Duplicate tourist permit in case of lose
- Cancellation of tourist permit

Figure 5.1

Tax assessment and collection from new motor vehicles

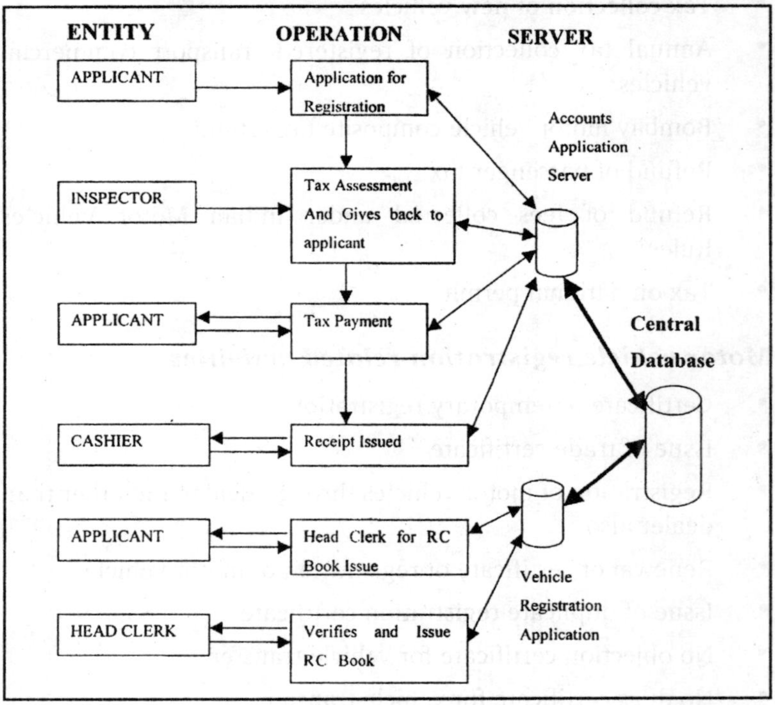

Issue of permits at RTO

- Contract carriage permit
- Goods carriage permit
- Temporary permit
- Special permit
- Private service vehicle permit
- Stage carriage permit
- National permit
- Duplicate permits in case of lose
- Transfer of permit
- Change of address in permit

Figure 5.2
Tax assessment and collection from registered commercial vehicles

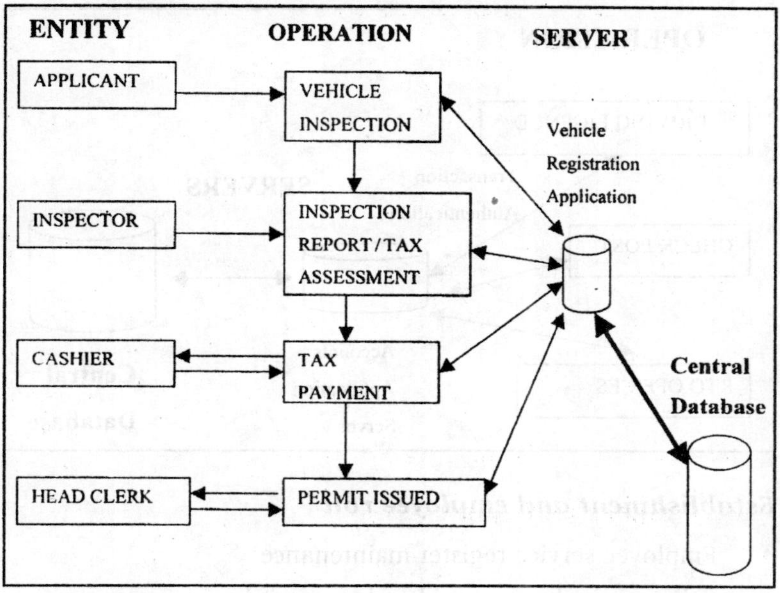

Departmental actions

- Departmental action cases clearance
- Prosecution case maintenance
- Fatal accident case register maintenance
- Departmental action cases remarks
- No departmental action case certificate issue

Check-post activities

- Collection of composite fees, tax and fines if any under Bombay Motor Vehicles Act
- Issue of temporary permits to transport vehicles
- Collection of departmental action fines
- Collection of penalty for overloading
- Daily cash collection maintenance

Figure 5.3
Accounts and audit trial

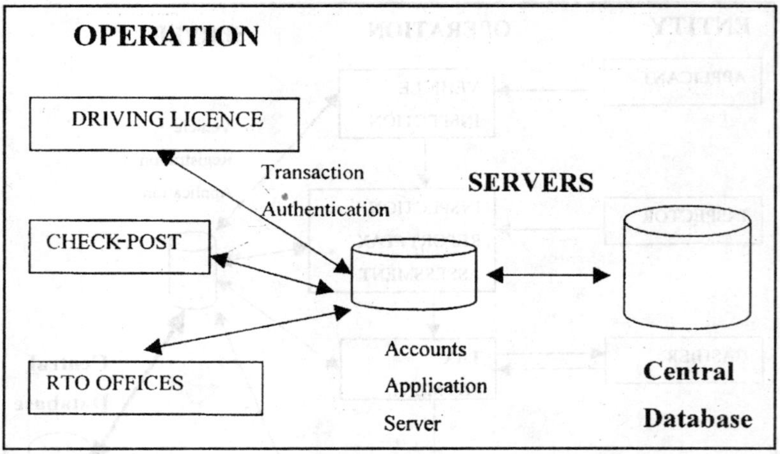

Establishment and employee roll

- Employee service register maintenance
- Salary and advances paid and recovered
- Disciplinary proceedings details
- Departmental audit details and compliances
- Accountant General audit details and compliances

Procurement

Similar to that of inter-state border check-posts projects, the stakeholder consultation process was undertaken to design the IMIS. The core team consisting of representatives from Transporters' Association, Deputy Director, Inspectors, senior employees from accounts and administration after a series of consultative meetings agreed upon a fully automated system where public-related operations are concerned. The emphasis was on eliminating wherever possible and minimizing in other parts the customer-employee interface. The discretion of the officers was also to be minimized.

Accordingly, bids were invited seeking total solution for MIS covering all the activities of the Transport Department as mentioned above. Pre-bid meetings were also held twice with a fortnight gap to explain the scope of work and to clear any doubt before submitting the bids.

A Technical Expert Committee, consisting of Secretary, Information Technology, Secretary, Transport Department, and technical experts from IIM, Ahmedabad, NIC and INDEXT-B was formed to evaluate the technical competency of the bidders. In all, four bidders responded and they were called to make a technical presentation before the committee. After their detailed technical presentation, all four were found qualified and recommended to open a commercial bid. The work was awarded to L-1 bidder (lowest commercial bid) who happens to be an Ahmedabad-based company and already had experience in developing software in other government offices. The Purchase Committee of the Government of Gujarat duly considered the recommendation of the Technical Committee and recommended to L-1 bidder.

Implementation

System requirements

Contrary to the earlier system of going to RTO, ARTO, inspectors and the agent etc., here the applicant has to go to only one specific counter. Accordingly, separate counters were designed as per the functions in all RTO offices with LAN connectivity. Once the applicant fulfils the pre-determined parameters, the higher archival steps are eliminated and the system issues the electronic sign approval or permit authorized by inspector in line with the Indian Motor Vehicles Act.

These processes were continued for all modules related to the motor vehicle but the internal processes also were designed user-friendly after the due consultation with the stakeholders (officers and employees of different levels). This divided the number of applications into two parts—one customer-related (external process) and the other employee-related (internal process).

Table 5.1
Application modules

Customer-related modules (external interface)	*Employee-related modules (internal operations)*
Issue of driving licence	Case collection
Issue of RC book	Accounts
Issue of vehicle permit	Audit
Issue of tax assessment	Statistics
Tax collection	Inward-outward correspondences
Departmental action cases	Human resource management
Driving school permit	

Customer-related external processes

Highest priority was given to those modules, which directly delivered to the citizens. The parameters were built in such a way that no room was left for human intervention in the process. The citizens' application-wise counters are designed in an exclusive area where applicants sit comfortably and get the things done immediately. It also left very little discretion at the level of ARTO or RTO with a purpose to eliminate bad practices. Delay had been the major reason encouraging corrupt practices in RTO office employees and the agents. IT as a tool is leveraged to eliminate delay and to issue instant approvals, particularly when there is a constant growth of vehicles taking place.

Employee-related internal processes,

Accounting system requires extreme care as it consists of assessment, collection and reconciliation of tax. Due care has been taken in designing the data structure to prevent erosion of data. Automatic audit trial was built at every step of internal processes to ensure accuracy.

Table 5.2
Growth in vehicle population

Year	*Number*	*Percentage*
1998-99	4679793	11%
1999-2000	5190732	11%
2000-01	5576040	7%
2001-02	6007969	8%
2002-03	6508370	8%
2003-04	7087490	9%

Source: Commissioner of Transport, Government of Gujarat.

Maintenance of different registers

All registers will be maintained by the system automatically as and when the data will be entered. The registers to be maintained are as follows:

- Court Stamp Cancel Register
- Inward-Outward Register
- Postal Stamp Register
- Personal Cash Register
- Demand Draft Register
- NP Checking Register
- Wanted Register
- Tax Wanted Register
- Cash Register
- Master Cash Register
- Dead Stock Register

System overview

At the headquarters, activity based individual application servers were configured as a security measure and were connected to the main server. A parallel server is also maintained in RTO office, Ahmedabad, in case of damage to the main server. The smart card driving licence system, computerized automation of inter-state border RTO check-posts and smart optical card RC book are also connected with the main server.

A central database was originally planned for "DB-2" from IBM as RDBMS. However, a small conflict related to conversion of data led to closure of the contract with IBM. Later, it was negotiated with ORACLE. They accepted to make this project as showcase. Hence ORACLE Enterprises (9i) was installed as RDBMS.

Network connectivity with all field offices was provided through 64 kbps telephone leased line. Switch-based routers from CISCO were used to establish the network connectivity from the

Figure 5.4
Application system overview

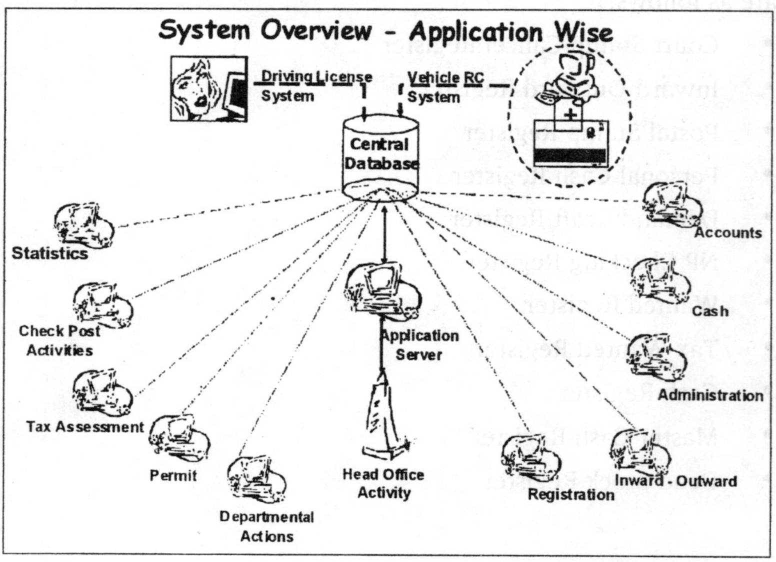

Figure 5.5

WAN connections from field offices and check-posts

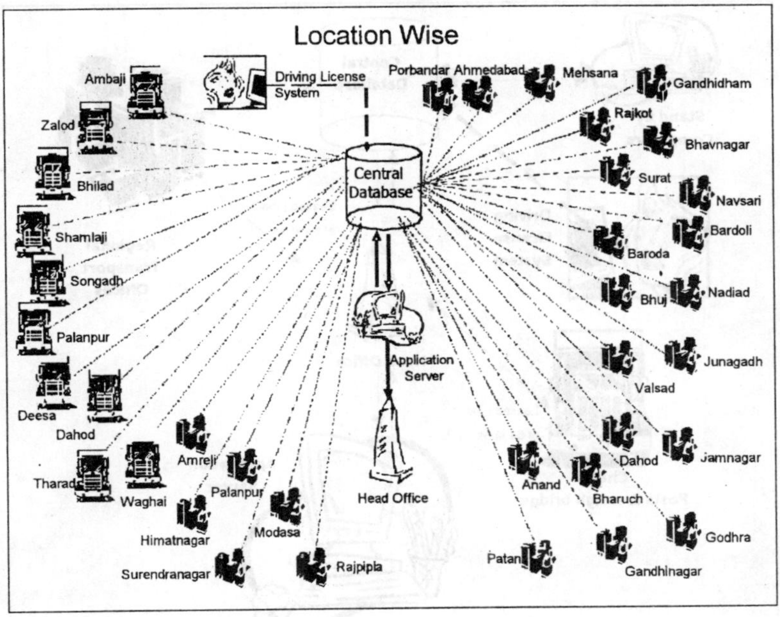

field office to application servers at head office and from there to the main server and the parallel server. Risk servers from IBM were originally configured as main server and parallel server with additional memory capabilities. Later, it was changed to Sun server as main and parallel server.

The system architecture was designed in such a way that the local office continues to get online and current MIS of all activities. Because of limitation on the network capacity in transacting graphic data etc., it was designed that field offices update every application server once in 24 hours (basically during peak hours). But the application servers are designed to automatically update the main server as soon as it gets the data from the field offices. Primarily, the LAN system was widely used whereas the WAN system was used carefully as per the requirement of priority data. This was done because of the limited 64 kbps telephone lines.

Figure 5.6
System network

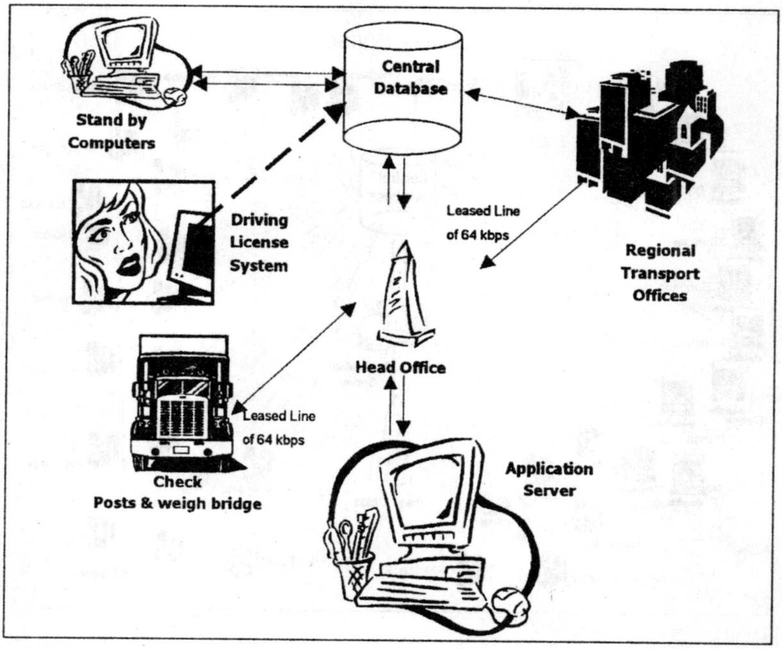

Security of the system

The system architecture was designed only as Intranet and there is no Internet facility given at all. Thus, any external entry into the system through Internet is not possible. The software were written in four sets of programmes so that whoever would like to venture to penetrate the system need to have all four sets of programme. Further, the programmes were encrypted in 32 bit, which makes it very difficult to break into an operator system unless the person is duly authorized by biometric identification. Every operator is authorized through biometric identification at different levels. The higher archival bureaucratic structure clearly defines the level of authority and accordingly the authorization was installed as a security measure. All the nodes at the counter were not provided with CVR floppy windows so that external entry into the system was totally prohibited.

Issues in implementation

At Transport Commissioner's office, after taking all precautions, the system architecture, system development and DBMS were configured immediately after the vendor was selected. But, a new problem was created. Since the vendor quoted L1 (lowest price of Rs. 43 lakh only), he was not able to employ more than two software engineers and was prolonging the work. They insisted on payment at every small stage. Time was not given to complete the project at all offices even though the Commissioner and his team did all system configurations and hardware configurations. After persisting efforts, the company could write only one set of programmes for all applications on which a trial run was done in the month of August 2000.

The RTO, Ahmedabad office started performing operations with the new system although it was a trial run, but by the transfer of the then Transport Commissioner in January 2001, all the activities came to a standstill. The system was reactivated again in the middle of year 2003, as the government was keen to streamline all the e-governance projects. However, expected success could not be achieved as use of the system was far from its designed capacity.

Difficulties in system integration

Lot of changes were taking place in all sectors of the Transport Department in a short time. Suddenly, all the employees became active and started getting involved in reform processes. But, a few senior officers had to retire one by one from the service, which left a gap in sharing the knowledge of how the flow charts and design systems were made by involvement of the employees. Further, inter-conflicts between the vendors of different projects also created misunderstanding and led to delay in implementation of linked project like DBMS. However, every project had been developed as stand-alone project. Therefore, integration of DBMS of different modules did not affect much, except delay the implementation.

Employees' understanding of computer operations had also been a major problem. Intensive training on computer familiarization improved the understanding and helped the implementing agencies as the employees sat along with them while programmes were being written. Enormous amounts of internal information were available to the programme writers, which helped the system to remove redundancies.

The networking through 64 kbps telephone lines had been a problem because of slow transaction of graphics from the check-posts. However, diluted resolutions of graphics and faster communication of digital data did not affect the daily functions and updating of data.

Benefits

As can be seen from the table and figure below, revenue started increasing from all the offices. Not only the tax revenue but also the composite fees like penalties from departmental action cases and overloading also substantially increased. Faster communication and immediate verification of vehicles registration and tax details through online system improved the speed of vehicle clearance. Every transaction is recorded and maintained, hence the transporters were very happy as they could get clear accounts from the drivers. While, the satisfaction level of transporters went high because of reduced roadside harassments, the employees' satisfaction also went high because of reduced level of possibilities of action from anti-corruption officials. The overall working environment became user-friendly and the major gain was to the government.

Conclusion

ICT applications covering all the three major activities of the Transport Department; smart card driving licence system, inter-state border transport check-posts and smart optical card registration certificate book were of the state-of-art. In some way, all the three applications were first of their kind in the world.

Table 5.3

Increase in income

	Name of the Office	1997-98	1998-99	1999-00	2000-01	2001-02	2002-03	2003-04
1	Ahmedabad	6330.64	6623.00	9028.49	7952.23	7115.34	8835.71	9711.09
2	Mahesana	1613.02	1962.24	2497.70	1776.60	1634.51	1851.07	2005.10
3	Patan				354.68	423.75	614.74	681.73
4	Rajkot	2561.55	2819.30	3305.44	3654.53	3318.22	4247.07	4879.48
5	Bhavnagar	1081.92	1300.09	1726.80	1809.59	1323.61	1890.49	2335.84
6	Surat	2855.92	3337.01	4349.44	4415.26	4583.22	5870.08	6818.87
7	Vadodara	3374.56	3753.97	4879.68	4684.01	4068.12	5082.97	5711.67
8	Nadiad	1643.63	1792.83	2437.54	2112.78	1873.83	2301.79	1646.04
9	Anand	0.00	0.00	0.00	0.00	0.00	0.00	1317.38
10	Palanpur	553.05	742.19	975.69	815.34	1022.95	1160.28	1293.63
11	Himmatnagar, Modasa	1080.30	1348.13	1527.03	1276.33	1207.97	1300.26	1517.17
12	Jamnagar	1285.08	1648.67	1979.20	1864.33	1924.06	2172.00	2255.81
13	Junagadh	1398.79	1598.22	1136.02	1105.68	1430.59	1464.28	1734.98
14	Porbandar	0.00	0.00	775.69	837.00	1012.04	973.08	944.64
15	Bhuj, Ghandhidham	2050.20	2426.92	2866.65	2727.81	3521.34	4148.16	4575.38

Contd...

Contd...

16	Surendranagar	462.98	560.57	650.98	557.61	697.67	833.10	953.30
17	Amreli	489.59	576.05	706.39	831.27	736.94	1120.17	1470.47
18	Valsad	1343.74	1534.28	1583.83	1387.22	1533.60	1799.21	2067.62
19	Bharuch	1104.19	1309.79	1731.07	1665.92	1542.37	1891.03	1971.01
20	Godhra	731.90	862.46	1070.16	985.53	847.23	1019.06	1075.66
21	Gandhinagar	350.47	512.90	907.74	1021.95	1303.02	1646.56	2144.79
22	Bardoli	596.35	689.65	808.92	758.48	728.64	970.36	1080.55
23	Dahod	293.34	347.79	377.48	356.19	303.36	356.72	404.47
24	Navsari	0.00	0.00	609.36	639.75	783.49	1008.35	1212.53
25	Rajpipla						106.27	209.60
1	Bhilad (CP)	941.01	1591.72	2636.49	3925.73	5088.16	5073.80	5728.77
2	Shamlaji (CP)	641.39	1228.94	1926.46	3379.14	4611.68	4713.50	4988.41
3	Songadh (CP)	309.00	687.22	1224.84	2286.12	3580.93	3986.22	4660.47
4	Amirgadh (CP)	335.31	705.40	1253.80	2345.00	3045.74	2353.63	2607.16
5	Deesa (CP)	262.22	652.97	1068.95	1659.00	2087.48	2846.54	2785.30
6	Dahc.. (CP)	248.23	318.17	572.16	905.99	1100.47	1119.23	1423.92
7	Zalod (CP)	40.11	56.03	110.62	128.04	143.77	151.29	197.62
8	Tharad (CP)	56.58	165.86	345.81	435.42	654.66	851.70	1275.15

Contd...

Contd...

9	Ambaji (CP)	222.93	198.70	170.81	196.15	212.45	235.09	256.95
10	Samakhiyali (CP)	0.00	0.00	0.00	1307.44	3108.49	2787.65	3801.30
11	Waghai(CP)	51.72	57.39	77.58	83.70	105.63	129.34	158.92
12	Jamnagar (CP)						636.31	1058.70
13	Chhota Udepur							140.80
14	Bhavnagar, Alang							351.27
	TOTAL (RTO/ARTO)	31201.20	35746.10	45931.30	43000.10	42935.90	52662.60	60018.80
	TOTAL (CP)	3108.50	5662.40	9387.52	16651.70	23739.50	24884.30	29083.50
	INCOME (COT)	8926.20	9627.10	13349.40	6266.40	11834.80	3633.97	21576.08
	GRAND TOTAL	43235.90	51035.60	68668.20	65918.30	78510.10	81180.90	110678.40

Figure 5.7
Increase in income

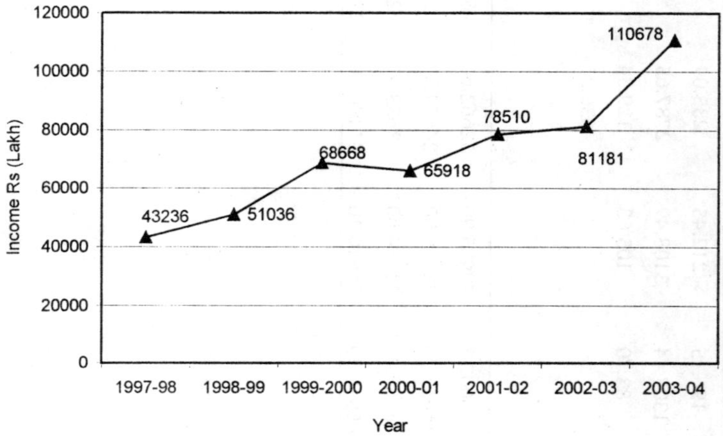

Integrating them and covering other supporting activities through an MIS was a logical extension and provided much needed efficiency improvement in the functioning of Transport Department. Substantial increase in revenue streams subsequent to the implementation of the ICT applications provide adequate proof for the success of the project.

6

Urban E-Governance

Ahmedabad Municipal Corporation (AMC) is one of major reform initiators among the urban local bodies in the country. The author was appointed from the Department of Transport to the AMC as Municipal Commissioner in the year 2001. The first few weeks of assessment showed that despite Ahmedabad's generally accepted image of well-governed city, the system required to be more transparent, accountable, and bring in citizen focus. The experience in Transport Department had proved worthwhile in improving the responsiveness and transparency among all the stakeholders. Therefore, without any hesitation, the decision was made to go in for e-governance application in AMC. Given the complexity of urban management, where over 40,000 employees are involved in attending to the needs of 3.5 million people, the task was more challenging. But, the system developed over a period of eight months proved to be citizen-centric and user-friendly in many ways. It is explained here how the project was implemented where transaction from birth to death is made possible through Internet.

Ahmedabad city: An overview

Ahmedabad is the largest city in the state of Gujarat and is also the seventh largest city in India. It is the commercial capital of the state. The city's development was from the establishment of.

textile mills in 1857. Textile industry was the backbone of its economy till two decades back. Today, Ahmedabad is a major industrial and financial city contributing about 14 percent of the total investments in all stock exchanges in India. The city, accounting for over 7 percent of total state population (2001), is estimated to contribute about 18 percent of the state income (see Table 6.1).

Table 6.1

Ahmedabad: Area and population growth

Census year	*Area (in sq km)*	*Population*	*as % of Gujarat*	
			Area	*Population*
1901	14.93	185889	0.008	2.04
1911	23.08	216777	0.012	2.21
1921	23.96	274007	0.012	2.69
1931	25.29	382768	0.013	3.33
1941	52.47	591267	0.027	4.32
1951	52.47	837163	0.027	5.15
1961	92.98	1149918	0.047	5.57
1971	92.98	1585544	0.047	5.94
1981	98.15	2059725	0.050	6.04
1991	190.84	2876710	0.097	6.96
2001	190.84	3515361	0.097	6.95

Source: Census of India (respective years).

The area under AMC's limit is spread over 190.84 sq km and accommodates 3.5 million people. Suburbs of 150 sq km with about one million people also live on the support of AMC civic services. AMC is divided into five zones, which are further divided into 43 wards.

Ahmedabad Municipal Corporation

Ahmedabad Municipal Corporation was constituted in July 1950 under Bombay Provincial Municipal Corporations Act (BPMC

Act), 1949. Further, the governance of urban local bodies (ULBs) assumes importance in the wake of the 74th Constitution Amendment Act, 1992 which delegates mandatory elections and greater devolution of powers and functions to the city corporations.

The BPMC Act provides for functions, duties and responsibilities to be carried out by the municipal corporations. These are divided into two categories—obligatory and discretionary. The obligatory functions include provision of water supply, drainage, streetlighting, sanitation, solid waste management, fire services, etc., as per section 63 of the Act. The discretionary functions include transportation facilities, construction and maintenance of secondary schools and technical institutions, construction and maintenance of rest houses, hospitals, markets, etc., generation and distribution of electricity or gas as per section 66 of the Act.

The Act also specifies what taxes a municipal corporation can levy and how they are to be charged. No powers for determining their own taxation structure exist with the corporation. Any change in taxation structure needs permission from the state government.

Governing structure of AMC

The governing structure of AMC consists of both political and administrative wings. The political wing is an elected body of councillors headed by the mayor. In order to deliver and implement civic services, a senior civil service officer deputed by the state government functions as the Municipal Commissioner of the AMC.

As per the BPMC Act, the powers are vested with four distinct statutory authorities of the elected wing, which are the General Board, Standing Committee, Transport Committee and School Board Committee. The General Board is the supreme body of the corporation with the mayor as its chairman. The Board takes all policy decisions. It approves the budget, sanctions appointments and expenditure estimates sent by various departments. The corporation has several statutory and non-statutory functional committees too.

Elected wing

The elected wing consists of municipal councillors elected by the citizens and the total number of councillors is related to the total population. At present, the AMC has 129 councillors elected from 43 wards. A deputy mayor assists the mayor and is elected from amongst the councillors. The term of both the mayor and his deputy is for a period of two-and-a-half years as per the newly amended provision in the Act.

Administrative wing

The Municipal Commissioner is the head of the administrative wing. The various departments under him have been divided amongst eight Deputy Municipal Commissioners. The organizational structure of the administrative wing is presented in Figure 6.1.

The administration has been decentralized into five zones, each of which are headed by a Deputy Municipal Commissioner. Their main responsibility is to look after the zonal functions of health and engineering departments but apart from that they are also endowed with the additional responsibility of coordination, guidance and policy decisions of city functions of each zone. The health department at the zonal level is responsible for food inspection, Branch Licence Permit, vaccination, birth/death registration, family planning, etc. While the engineering department is responsible for building new roads up to 60 feet, widening roads, repairs and resurfacing, constructing new buildings, maintaining municipal properties, sanctioning water connections, carrying out repairs of water pipelines, removing encroachments etc. Other three Deputy Municipal Commissioners are in charge of only the city functions of finance, engineering and solid waste management. No zonal responsibilities have been given to them.

Figure 6.1

Organizational structure of the administrative wing of AMC

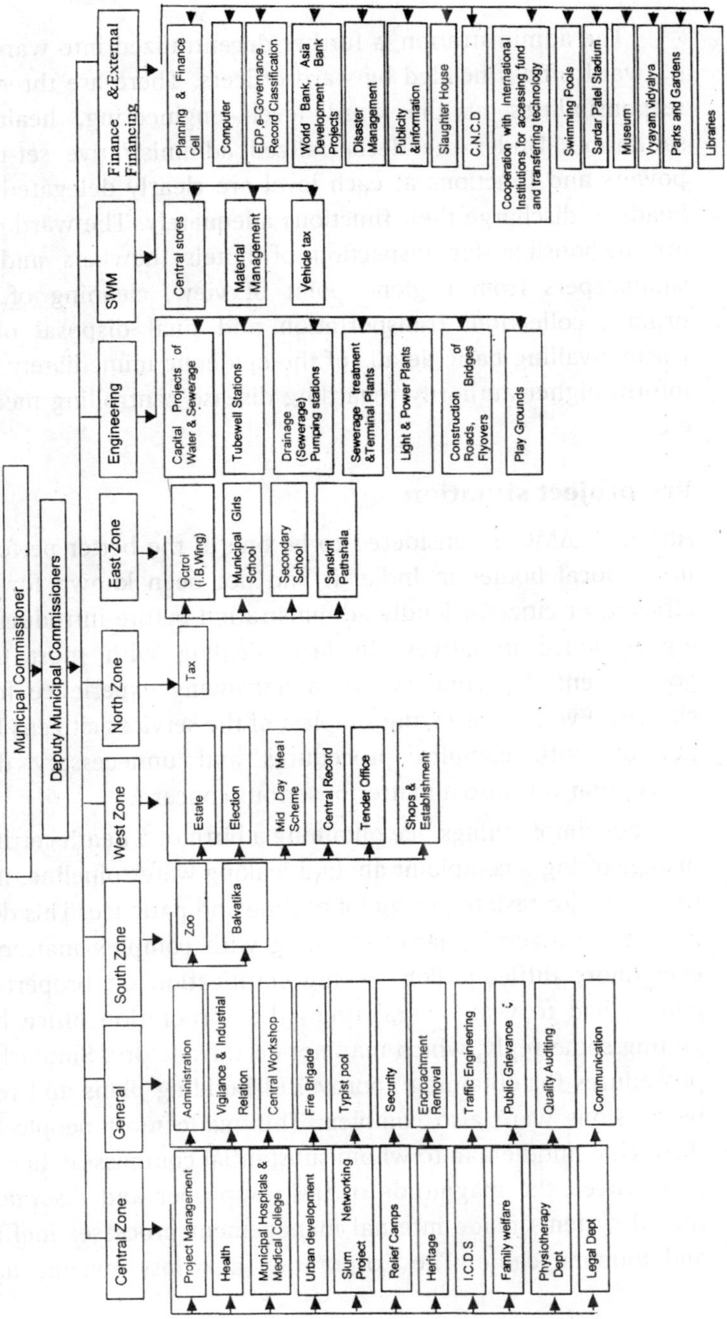

The administration is further decentralized into wards with 43 ward offices headed by ward officers. There are three major responsibilities at the ward level—engineering, health and sanitation. Under the decentralized administrative set-up, the powers and functions at each level are clearly delegated to the heads to discharge their functions adequately. The ward officers are responsible for inspection of hotels, hawkers and small shopkeepers from hygiene point of view, cleaning of public urinals, collection, transportation and final disposal of solid waste, availing basic details of the epidemic immediately and to inform higher authority regarding disease controlling measures, etc.

Pre-project situation

Although AMC is considered to be one of the better performing urban local bodies in India, it had not been known for either efficient or citizen-friendly administration before introduction of e-governance initiatives: In fact, dealing with most of the government departments was a harrowing experience for the citizens. Even for receiving simplest of the services citizens had to put up with complex procedures and unnecessary delays. Corruption was also a matter of serious concern.

For simple things like obtaining a birth or a death certificate, or registering a complaint about a leaking water pipeline, it used to be a major task requiring lot of time and patience. This despite having a Citizens' Charter! Dealing with complex matters was even more difficult. For seeking clarification on property tax, people had to visit several times the corporation office before getting some reply, which may not be satisfactory. Similarly, the procedures for obtaining approval of building plans and related permissions were also complex. This made most people to go through a middleman to whom substantial commission had to be paid. Given the magnitude of task, improper and disorganized record systems made internal management processes inefficient and unmanageable. The Corporation also lost revenue due to inefficient collection system. This resulted in a perpetual vicious circle where inadequate revenue led to limits on system upgradation and recruitment, which in turn to inadequate services.

Problems in existing system

The general impression about government offices in a developing nation—as is true all over the world—is that government costs too much, delivers too little and is not sufficiently responsive or accountable. Good governance reforms aim to address these shortcomings and perform better. Essentially, the role of a local urban government body is to contribute to the economic development of the city. At the same time, all citizens, who are the taxpayers, should be treated like customers and should get the benefits of economic development and better civic amenities without any problems.

In AMC, like most of the government organization, there did not exist a system with which the citizens could instantly know which relevant department of AMC they had to pay or address/redress for complaints. There was also a need of strong mechanism to arrest tax evasion and to widen the tax base. It was found that rampant corruption among employees and the elected members was the main deterrent factor, which did not allow changes for better. Therefore, it was necessary to encourage people for a better management system and the challenge was to influence the behaviour of all three stakeholders, viz., the employees, the elected councillors and the citizens of the city.

Reform measures required

To bring in overall reforms of the system and functions, there was a primary requirement to understand the role of all stakeholders of the organization and evolve a public awareness campaign similar to that of a commercial marketing campaign. This would call for a greater participation of all stakeholders in re-engineering the processes through a well-planned change management strategy and mass communication skills. Visual and print media needed to be used to bring in awareness among citizens of their rights, involve employees in the re-engineering process and motivate them to accept social responsibility and seek more cooperation from the elected members of the AMC for system changes. These three stakeholders had to play an important role to bring in transparent system, simple procedures, increased revenue collection, increased environment awareness, education on water use and sanitation etc. In order to achieve these, social marketing techniques were extensively used to replace the old system.

Vicious circle of stakeholders

The internal relationship between the three stakeholders is traditional, existing on conflicting interests and pressures on each other as shown in Figure 6.2 below:

Figure 6.2
Stakeholders vicious circle

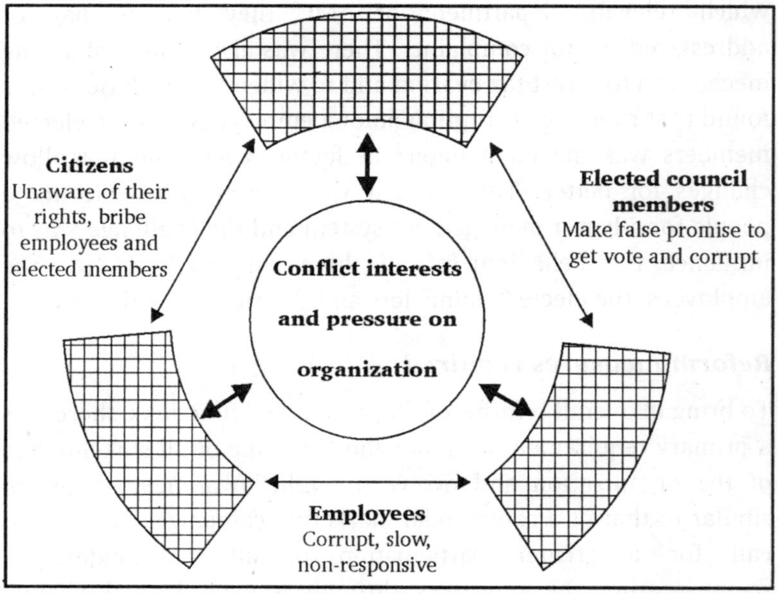

Citizens

Citizens, being the primary beneficiary of the organization and unaware of their rights, are bribed by employees and elected members to get their work done. A few vested interests among citizens indulge in bad practices to get favours, which are not legally possible. These only widen the scope for more malpractices and corruption. Slow and manual systems were not equipped to arrest such malpractices. Honest citizens were left helpless and there was no appropriate forum to approach and redress.

Employees

Employees of AMC are the next major stakeholders as they deliver civic services to the citizens through the system and procedures designed by them. Lack of transparency in the system, and also lengthy procedures, did not have the capability to bring accountability in employees. Being urban local government, most of the employees were employed over a period of time by the undue influence of elected members and hence they had deceptive umbrella to protect them from their misdeeds. Poor control mechanism and lengthy disciplinary proceedings encouraged the employees to be irregular and indifferent to their work.

Elected members

The elected members have five-year term. They are always in a hurry to be popular so as to ensure their victory in the next election. To achieve this objective, they cannot afford to say 'no' to anyone for any kind of legal or illegal works. Brazenly, the elected members would support an illegal construction for pecuniary benefits or to be more popular among slum dwellers etc. The informal relationship with the employees helps them to extend undue favours.

The intricate internal relationship between above three stakeholders builds stress on the organizational structures, systems and resources, which ultimately makes the organization ineffective and weak. On the other side, the citizens, as customers to the corporate body of Ahmedabad Municipal Corporation, are the ultimate sufferers. Unaware of their involvement in this 'stakeholder vicious circle', the citizens hurt their own interests, economic activity and growth of the city. The organization is neither equipped itself to handle such customer dissatisfaction nor have any technique to measure customer satisfaction.

Need for a new system

Once the problems in the existing system were identified, the reform process was aimed to gain internal efficiency, improve citizen services and promote economic competitiveness (see Figure 6.3).

Figure 6.3
Objectives of the reform process

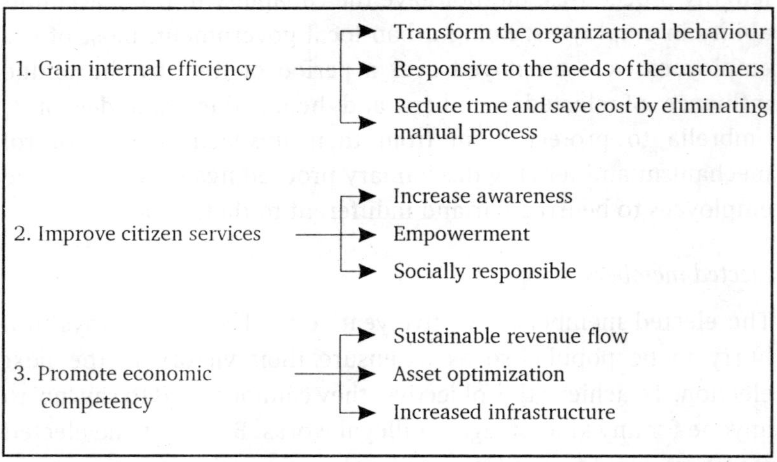

Solutions to achieve these objectives are to bring in organizational transformation using information technology for system correction and extensive use of internal marketing to change the attitudes of stakeholders (see figure 6.4).

Over and above, administrative management of AMC was a major problem. Application of modern computer technology for upgradation of AMC's administrative management and for its

Figure 6.4
Solutions

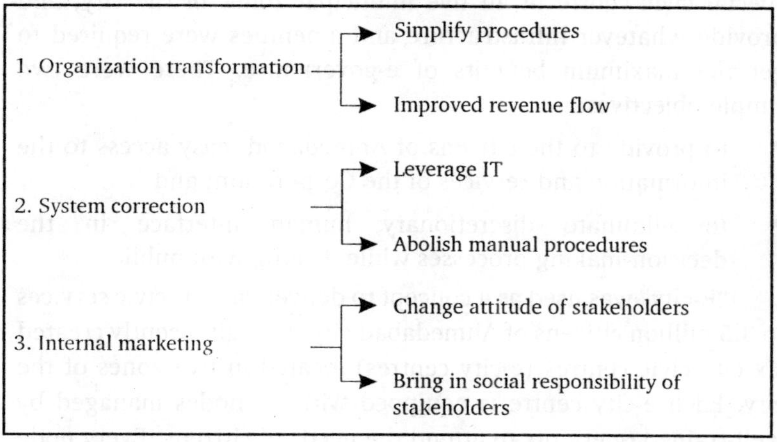

welfare activities was adopted as the right solution. A provision of Rs. 500 lakh was made for e-governance during the year 2002-03 with the help of state government.

E-governance: Initiation

There was a realization among the top management of AMC that the shortcomings of the existing system of information management were the main cause of inefficiencies, which indirectly encouraged bad practices. The decision was made to introduce comprehensive reforms in the functioning of the Corporation to make it more efficient, transparent and citizen-friendly.

Every citizen, right from birth registration to primary education, primary health, public transport, city cleanliness, water supply, sewerage, road, streetlights, parks and gardens and even for crematorium, needs to approach the Municipal Corporation. Therefore, to achieve the objectives of good governance, e-governance was seen as a way to provide easy access to information to the staff as well as citizens. It was decided to involve the employees from all departments of the Corporation for developing the proposed e-governance system. Another priority of the initiative was to make it as easy as possible for the citizens to interface with the AMC. Therefore, it was decided to set up a special civic centre in all five municipal zones of the city, and provide whatever infrastructure and amenities were required to get the maximum benefits of e-governance. There were two simple objectives:

- to provide to the citizens of Ahmedabad, easy access to the information and services of the Corporation; and
- to eliminate discretionary human interface in the decision-making processes while dealing with public.

"E-city" was used as a concept to deliver various civic services to 3.5 million citizens of Ahmedabad city through recently created six city civic centres (e-city centres) located in five zones of the city. Each e-city centre is equipped with 10 nodes managed by well-trained operators to attend the needs of citizens. Every node is equipped to deliver any activity either it is building plan permission or shops and establishment licence or complaints regarding civic amenities or payment of taxes etc. The operator processes the request of the citizens and issues necessary licences or receipts instantly.

Formation of task teams and preparation of flow charts

AMC has 42 different departments to constitute the task teams; two officers were drawn out from each department. The responsibility of the teams was to prepare step-wise charts of manual processes involved in delivering each service by the Corporation. These charts acted as the flow charts for every activity of each department. The task team for each department consisted of officers from different levels. The preparation of flow charts took almost seven months.

After the flow charts were prepared, AMC appointed a total solution provider (TSP) through Gujarat Informatics Ltd. (GIL). TSP's professional team (M/s Microtech Systems Ltd.) joined hands with AMC's task team to modify the flow charts. The purpose behind the whole exercise was to minimize the number of steps involved in the whole process and reduce time consumption.

Preparation of SRS document

Flow charts were modified, volume of data transactions were estimated, and the processes were defined. The information thus obtained became the framework for the preparation of SRS (system requirement specification) document. After going through the SRS document, the task teams further modified the steps suitably in order to make them more workable in designing the complete system. This took almost a month.

System design

After the system was designed, activity-wise programme software was prepared by the TSP. The entire exercise was carried out in the presence of the task team. This participatory approach helped TSP to come out with the software within one-month time.

Leadership-mobilizing stakeholders

The Municipal Commissioner of AMC was the main champion of this initiative. It was his firm conviction about the potential benefits of e-governance that gave the necessary push to this initiative. One of the Deputy Commissioners was given the responsibility for project development and implementation. He led the AMC teams who made this project a reality in little over a year. Since this project was implemented by a number of inter-departmental teams, the credit for good leadership also goes to various officers of AMC who worked as team leaders and continued to be involved in the operation of the system.

Involvement of the municipal employees throughout project preparation and implementation phase generated a feeling of ownership among them. The realization of their stake in the successful implementation of the project would become a factor of motivation for them to run the system with greater accountability.

AMC has 42 departments and two officers from each department were involved in the preparation of activity flow charts, which formed the foundation of this initiative. One of the main reasons for the successful development and implementation of this initiative was the large number of capable and committed staff of AMC who were deployed in this project.

System architecture

The project commenced in January 2002, and the first civic centre was inaugurated on September 18, 2002. Within a period of only eight months, e-governance was made available in the service of the people. The system has two different aspects:

(a) system for communication between the citizens and the Municipal Corporation, and
(b) system for Municipal Corporation's own use.

Both of the above systems provide several online facilities (see Figure 6.5). The system designed for the citizens' use enables them to access a wide range of online services. The system for the

Figure 6.5

AMC e-governance system architecture

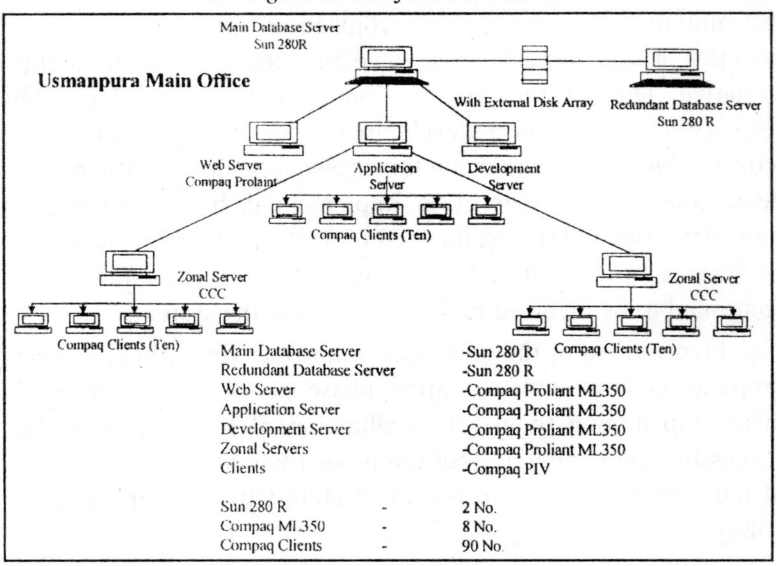

Figure 6.6
City civic centres

Figure 6.7
Location of six city civic centres

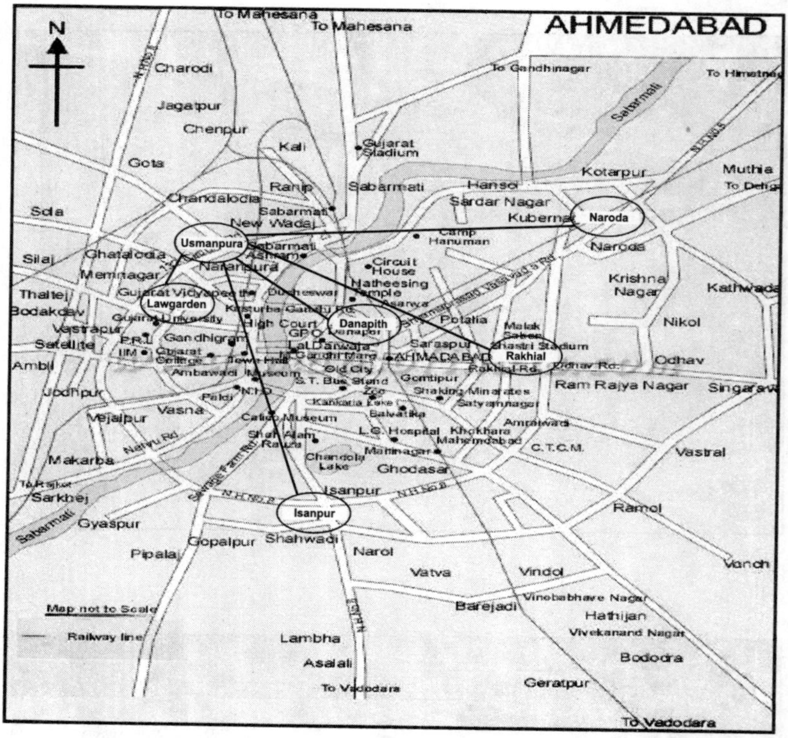

Corporation's internal use is serving as a Management Information System (MIS) for the municipal officials. The system enables the department heads to see the status of registered complaints. Official information and notices are circulated at once using the Intranet. Employees can also check the status of their Employee Provident Fund (EPF) online.

The six civic centres are interconnected as well as connected with the 43 municipal wards with an Intranet lease line (64 kbps). People can register complaints and grievances at any of these locations. Total cost of the project is estimated to be Rs. 152 lakhs, which includes all hardware, software and capital cost.

Details of e-governance project initiated by AMC in 2002

- It is a dream project undertaken with the help of Microtech System, having members from eight selected committees.
- Grant is provided by Gujarat Informatics for software part, of which Rs. 1 crore are already sanctioned.
- Main sections incorporated under the project are property tax, vehicle tax, certificates of birth and death and plan approval from TDO etc.
- There are six civic centres* having 10 nodes each in zonal offices (five administrative zones and one in old town). All of these are server zones, whereby total information is web-based and linked. One can calculate one's own tax online.
- Also, there is a complaint redressal department, which is an open system, where one can find out the status of his/her complaint.
- Operation and maintenance of the e-governance project is to be done by AMC, for which 650 officials have been trained by Microtech Systems Ltd.
- In the operational phase, each civic centre has 10 node operators, one system manager and one system operator.

Other sub-functions of the system:

- Float tenders online.
- Budgets for the ongoing financial year.
- To incorporate the current status of all infrastructure projects.
- Setting up kiosks at all civic centres.

Special features

Citizens are provided access to the city civic centres and the ward offices through a utility driven Internet website (www.egovamc.org or www.egovamc.com). Internet provides the

---

* Five more civic centres are being opened this month.

Figure 6.8
e-governance applications

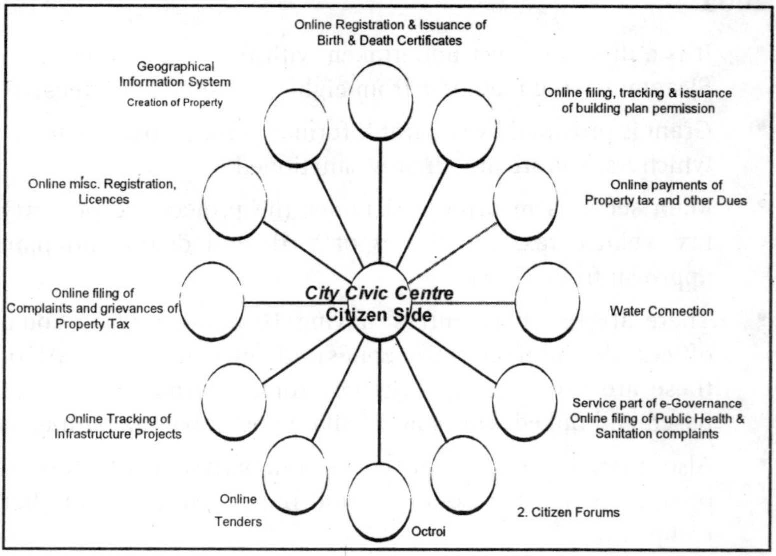

Figure 6.9
Resource utilization

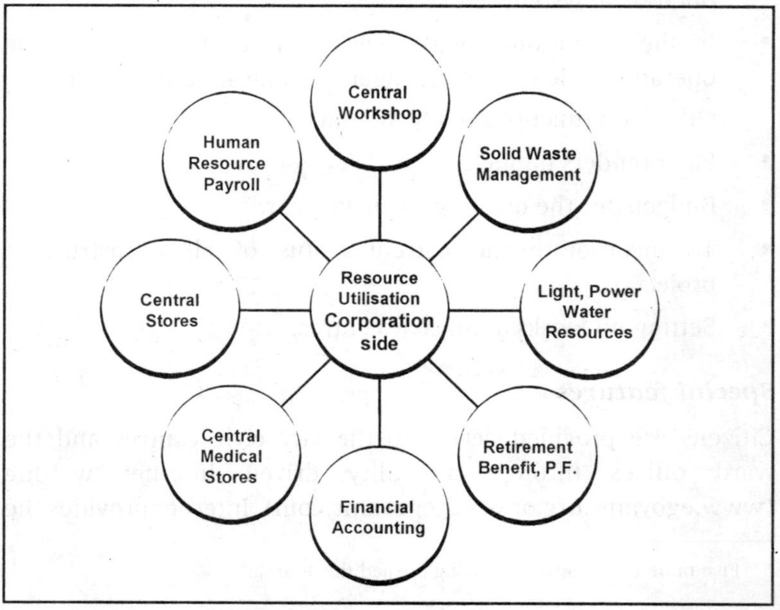

most cost-effective method of reaching people. It is a single window to gain access to AMC's Intranet and the LAN. The website also gives online information related to the assessment of property tax, related procedures and government rules, as well as the building rules and regulations. As the city civic centres are on the network connected to the main server, which in turn is connected through the global internet protocol, the citizens can track the status of their application through the website. One can also download forms related to shops and establishments, property tax assessment, water supply connections, land and estate, and birth and death registration.

Besides, services offered at the city civic centres are:

- Collection of property tax.
- Collection of vehicle tax.
- Registration of property tax changes/complaints.
- Issuance and renewal of trade licence (shop and establishment)
- Collection of sign board (advertisement).
- Issuance of building plan permission.
- General complaints registration.

Infrastructure

The total project cost (excluding civil works) was Rs. 250 million. This includes the cost of computer hardware, communication equipment and software development.

AMC's own buildings were modified and converted into civic centres. The incremental cost of civil works was not very large. All the civic centres are air-conditioned and are provided with the proper sitting arrangements for the visitors. Beautiful landscaping creates a pleasant ambience at the civic centres. The strategy of converting AMC's own assets into civic centres was a cost-effective approach to raise the required infrastructure.

It was decided to purchase the required computer hardware of best available brands in the country. The idea was to assure

Figure 6.10
Revenue from property tax

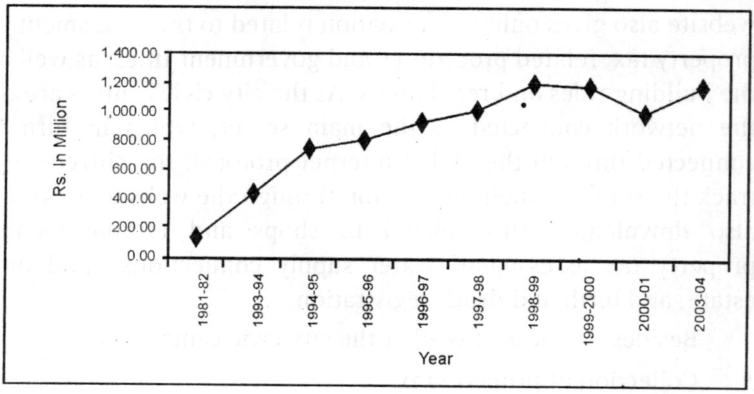

contract-free maintenance of the computer hardware on account of the warranty offered by the good companies on purchase of the hardware. Another reason for investing on branded hardware was its reliability. The entire hardware came with three-year manufacturer's warranty. Similarly, the TSP would continue to provide software support for the next three years under the existing contract.

Project implementation

The implementation of e-governance made the delivery of civic services a much easier task than before. In case of each of the following services, it drew several advantages ranging from increase in revenue to increased efficiency in the department:

Collection of property tax

The financial management of governments hinges on a sound, transparent, efficient and foolproof tax collection system. The method should provide ease and flexibility with which the citizens are able to pay their dues. Before the project was put into place, the citizens were required to go to the ward office, get in touch with the tax collector for calculating and preparing the payment receipts.

As the entire operation was done manually, searching through the records and carrying out the required calculations would invariably take time. In case, the tax collector was not present in the ward office, the citizens had to wait endlessly. The citizens also did not have any idea about the method of calculations in determining their dues. This led to resentment and made them to visit various AMC offices for such calculations. The system also led to volume of paper works at different levels entailing huge costs and time. The reconciliation of the revenue collection used to be a big time job and leave AMC to loose about Rs. 100 million per annum.

The simplified tax calculation system of all one million properties has been put on the web for public to access the calculation method of property tax of any property in the city, and other related details about the property etc. The manual exercise of calculations has been replaced by automated calculations and the AMC is now able to assess real-time demand and collection of property tax.

Table 6.2

Property tax collection through city civic centres (1 Apr 03 to 31 Mar 04)

Civic Centre	*Transactions*	*Amount (Rs)*
Law Garden	39,420	14,47,34,924.09
MEMCO	89,455	23,42,51,926.60
Maninagar	73,303	16,18,80,760.07
Rakhial	80,338	19,91,59,321.50
Usmanpura	93,703	38,29,90,057.19
Sardarbaug	51,189	13,18,76,919.65
Danapith	68,975	23,66,45,006.90
ICICI web	28	57,035.00
Bank	10,611	2,83,57,649.00
Total	5,07,022	1,51,99,53,600.00

Table 6.3
Property tax transaction and collection through banks and webs (1 Apr 03 to 19 Feb 04)

	Transactions	*Amount (million Rs)*
ICICI web	27	.038
Banks	10,491	28.1
Total	10,518	28.2

Payment of motor vehicle tax

AMC has connected its systems with the RTO office and octroi check-posts. This enables an effective check on evasion of vehicle tax. Collection of municipal lifetime vehicle tax has been decentralized and citizens can now pay this tax at any of the six civic centres. Payments can also be made through credit card. Facility of online payment of motor vehicle tax is also available.

ICICI Bank as backend for finance and accounts of AMC

The unique system wherein ICICI bank payment gateway was linked with AMC network to collect and make all payments, was developed. The system has considerably accelerated the process of transactions. For the Corporation, it has generated the goodwill and faith of the citizens, builders, contractors and other sections of the society dealing with it.

Now, people do not have to stand in a long queue as tax can be paid at any of the six civic centres. Easy access to information and online payment facility through credit card or infinity payment gateway of ICICI Bank has reduced the tax evasion and increased the collection. Other local banks are also connected with AMC's Intranet to collect taxes.

Online complaint registration system

All 43 wards are connected through Intranet and Internet to receive and redress complaints on civic services or matters related to municipal dues. The complainant gets a complaint number while registering, through which the status of the particular complaint and actions taken by the AMC can be tracked later. Citizens can also give feedback and suggestions online. The complaints filed online are directly received by the Commissioner and are automatically directed to the concerned officers and at the same time they are also transferred to the database. The database provides sufficient information to the department officials in carrying out rigorous monitoring of the actions taken for grievance settlement.

Table 6.4

Category-wise complaints summary
(1 Apr 03 to 19 Feb 04)

Category	*Received*	*Solved*	*Pending*
Octroi	19	3	16
Dead animal removal	88	76	12
Illegal construction	522	137	385
Streetlights	830	806	24
Water	4406	4378	28
Drainage	49707	49547	160
Storm water drainage	103	103	0
Roads and footpaths	4548	4522	26
Public buildings	188	185	3
Health	3893	3786	107
Encroachments	236	28	208
Others	1035	295	740
Total	65575	63866	1709

Online building plan approvals

All city civic centres are equipped to conduct instant scrutiny and issue approval of building plans through predetermined parameters as stipulated by the General Development and Control Regulations (GDCR). Buildings other than commercial establishments or high-rise buildings are given permissions on the spot.

Figure 6.11
Public convenience

THE ASIAN AGE 28 DECEMBER 2002

You can now file AMC complaint from Finland

[illegible]

The Times of India, Ahmedabad

Saturday, December 28, 2002

Online civic service a boon for Amdavadis

TIMES NEWS NETWORK

Ahmedabad: Very few took Ahmedabad municipal commissioner P Panneervel seriously when he said six months back that many civic services would be available to over 35 lakh Amdavadis online.

And today, the Ahmedabad Municipal Corporation (AMC) can boast of being the only civic body in the country to have total e-governance solutions. Be it general complaints, property tax collection, issuance of trade licence or granting building plan permission, things were never so easy for the common man and the 'babus' sitting across the table.

"The online system helps us in checking minute details of a building plan submitted in an instant, unlike manually sifting through piles of records earlier," says Kamlesh Patel, a TDO sub-inspector at the Usmanpura civic centre.

The new system has also ushered in a new work culture among civic employees. It also helps us spare a part of the workforce for the speedy execution of other services at the ground level, adds Patel.

In a period of just four months the new online system transacted over 84,500 cases at the Law Garden, Naroda, Maninagar, Rakhial, Usmanpura and the Sardarbaug civic centres. The internet was also used simultaneously for the collection of about Rs 16.36 crore in property and other taxes by the civic body.

Interestingly, citizens residing on both the sides of the Sabarmati accepted the e-revolution taking place in the civic body. The Usmanpura civic centre handled the maximum of 19,714 cases, mopping Rs 5.15 crore in the process. This was followed by the Naroda centre with over 16,274 cases and a collection of Rs 2.36 crore.

According to Panneervel and his team, the volume of work done during these four months in all the five civic centres, including through the internet, was better than the manual procedure. "The entire system is hacker proof and is designed to store data and expansion plans for the next 50 years," claims Panneervel.

The online e-governance system also helped in the speedy processing of general complaints received at the civic centres and via the internet. The Usmanpura centre disposed of 1,342 cases against the 1,543 received, leaving a backlog of just 201. Internet users in the city and around the world posted the maximum number of complaints.

Of the 10,422 complaints received by the central data server via the internet so far, only 320 complaints are still pending.

Municipal Commissioner P Panneervel demonstrating to journalists the online building plan approval system at the new City Civic Centre in Ahmedabad on Friday.

The process of approving building plan has been re-engineered and the whole responsibility that the plan conforms to existing byelaws is on the professional. If AMC inspector finds any discrepancy during site inspection, a heavy penalty is imposed and the professional's registration with the AMC is cancelled. Earlier, any building permit would take a week upto a few months to be issued. This process has not only decreased time, but also made the system more realistic.

Citizens can see or download the GDCR from the website. The applications can also be downloaded and submitted online. Details of the structural engineers registered with the AMC is also available on the website of AMC. The facility of online tracking the status of the application is also available.

Licence for shops and establishments

The civic centres issue licences for shops and establishments instantly. Renewal of the licence is also carried out across the counter. The process earlier was not very transparent and involved the discretion of the staff involved.

Through the database for online registration, the system enables the AMC to collect fees for signboards and hoardings. It was difficult to carry out and monitor this task manually before e-governance was introduced in the city.

Table 6.5

Transactions made through city civic centres
(between 18 Sept 02 to 31 Mar 04)

Application	*No. of transactions*	*Amount*
Birth applications	318	13,625
Death applications	221	20,375
Birth and death	1,317	57,500
Building plan	1,687	87,149,538
Property tax	4,69,702	1,385,231,587
Shops and establishments	17,703	1,546,679
TDOFEE	3,224	36,407,930
Vehicle tax	12,848	9,524,259

Instant issuance of birth and death certificates

The website of AMC provides access to all hospitals to register the births and deaths online. The application for registration of birth or death can also be downloaded from the website.

Earlier, the entire operation of collecting the information from the hospitals and maintaining it in the muster records used to take enormous time. The citizens were to ensure that the concerned ward offices send the correct data to the Corporation's central office to make entry in the registration book. The manual record-keeping makes impossible to search and deliver the certificates in a limited time. Now, the e-governance project registers and delivers the certificate instantly through city civic centres. The applications for registration of the births and deaths also can be downloaded from the website. With the help of this system, citizens can get the certificate instantly on demand.

Online information of infrastructure works and tenders

The process of issuing tenders, sanctioning of infrastructure works and processing within the organization has been computerized. The entire module is also linked to the website so that the citizens can access information regarding infrastructure works undertaken in the area.

The online information regarding infrastructure projects and related tenders in process could attract well-qualified contractors from all over the country. The payment procedures through bank-to-bank accounts has now reduced the procedural delay and increased the confidence of the contractors.

Engineering module

A unique module has been developed for planning and approval of all the projects and O&M works automatically by providing linkage with budget and fund availability. The annual budget for various categories allows ward officers to obtain necessary approvals through Intranet. The system has been planned to eliminate rampant indiscipline in the departments related to project planning and implementation.

Project impacts

Key benefits of the e-governance projects are:

- All departments are integrated.
- AMC is more responsive and transparent. Data retrievability has increased many times and it is very easy for the decision-makers to access and draw data.
- Chances for corruption are eliminated.
- Quicker service to citizens.
- 24-hour remote access to AMC transactions and services.
- Payment gateways and electronic transactions eliminate manual intervention.
- Higher revenue and enhanced cash flow.
- Better understanding and goodwill from citizens

Increase in revenues, time savings

Property tax collection

In 2002-03, the amount of property tax collected was Rs. 1,300 million, which is the highest ever for AMC. For the first time in the history of the AMC, the system has enabled it to close the tax account at the end of the year.

Octroi collection

AMC could make highest ever octroi collection of Rs. 3,630 million in the year 2002-03. It is expected that there will be an increase by 25 percent in the revenues from octroi collection after the complete automation of octroi stations.

Motor vehicle tax collection

Now, vehicle tax can be paid at any of the civic centres or at any octroi station. Increase in the number of collection centres has made the system more convenient for the taxpayers. This has also resulted in additional revenue of Rs.20 million from vehicle tax within six months.

ICICI Bank as backend for finance and accounts of AMC

The system has saved the leakage of at least Rs. 400 million per annum. It has brought down the tender quotes for projects by 10 percent on account of speedier payments from AMC's account to contractor's account in the same bank. The daily validations of cheques and payments have now reduced the huge loss incurred by the Corporation on account of lack of validation.

Sustainability of the initiative

Firstly, in terms of financial costs and returns, it is clear that the increase in revenues of the AMC as a result of this initiative far outweighs the project costs. So, the financial sustainability of the initiative is not in question. Secondly, the large number of transactions that have taken place at each of the civic centres is evidence of the citizens' positive response to this new format of service delivery. This adds to the project's sustainability.

The smart approach taken by the AMC to involve its own staff at every stage of project development has also resulted in operational sustainability of the new system.

There are certain features of the project, such as the tie-up with hospitals to provide daily information about births and deaths or with banks, for which sustainability is not guaranteed. However, it is safe to assume that these types of efficient business practices are here to stay both in the private sector as well as the public sector.

Following the example of the Ahmedabad Municipal Corporation, a small municipal council with a population of 1.43 lakh, which falls in Ahmedabad urban agglomeration, has also adopted the e-governance initiative. It is the first municipality in India to have a website or undertake e-governance.

Conclusion

The most important lesson of this initiative is that a smart approach for introducing IT-based e-governance system in an urban local body is to involve the staff in the system development. This strategy is more cost-effective than hiring external consultants to develop the system and then training the staff to operate it.

Another important lesson emerging from this initiative is that urban local bodies must realize that the old manual systems of administration lack transparency and are inherently inefficient because of information bottlenecks. The information technologies have created an extraordinary opportunity to provide efficient, transparent and responsive governance.

Finally, the increase in the revenue of AMC and the significant improvements in service delivery that have been realized by AMC, are evident of the cost-effectiveness of this initiative.

7

E-Learning in Ahmedabad Schools

The schoolnet project was the next attainment in the history of 'e-governance' implications in Gujarat. Though it was following the same path similar to e-governance in transport sector, a special value of 'social benefit' is attached with the schoolnet project. This difference is also visible when one analyzes the cost-benefit advantages of e-governance in transport projects vs schoolnet project. This chapter explains how the schoolnet project was implemented.

Ahmedabad Municipal Corporation (AMC) functions as per the Bombay Provincial Municipal Corporation Act, and the task of primary education within AMC limit comes under the obligatory functions of the Corporation.

There are total 563 public schools having 2.25 lakh children in the primary classes (June 2003). The total number of teachers is about 4,000 and budget for primary school education is about Rs. 110 crore per annum (9.1% of total budget of AMC). The growing awareness among people about education and special governmental efforts, like 'free education for girlchild', has increased the enrolment of students in municipal schools.

Pre-project scenario

Students' profile

Due to many reasons, majority of the children coming to municipal schools are from slum areas or from poor families. Most of parents are either illiterate or semi-literate. Some of the children also help their parents in earning their livelihoods. With this kind of background, the motivational aspects of these children in their academic pursuits are limited. However, there are quite a number of children who take initiatives and work hard to fulfil their academic pursuits. There are also examples of students from municipal schools appearing in the merit list and getting scholarships for higher secondary education.

Teaching aids/capabilities

AMC, being an urban local body, priorities are given to basic civic amenities like drinking water, sanitation etc. than primary education. The financial constraints also affect the resources allocation to primary education sector. Therefore, the schools are not well-maintained and teaching aids are bound to be inadequate.

In the absence of adequate equipment and teaching aids, the teachers do not equip themselves for quality teaching. The overall attitude is least professional and therefore the quality municipal school education is quite poor compared to other private schools in the city. This is also the reason why children completing primary education from the municipal schools are not compatible to the private school children. This also results into large dropouts from primary to secondary schools.

As far as the higher-level management is concerned, a committee consisting of elected councillors headed by a chairman is responsible to review the functioning of the schools. Here also, academic affairs get least priority due to high political components involved in the committee and things move at very slow pace.

Society outlook about the municipal schools

By and large, the education sector receives generous donations from local community, which is utilized by the private trust schools and NGOs. The basic perception about the municipal schools by the society is poor and they presume that political interventions by the local body councillors are high. Therefore, these primary schools receive only government funds for managing the school activities.

Further, commercialization of education is taking place right from the primary level all over the country. The children from affluent society pay very high fees to those schools, which teach them with modern equipment and amenities. This widens the gap in the educational understanding level of a municipal school student versus a private primary school student from same age group. Hence, equal opportunities for these children from the municipal schools are knocked out. However, there are larger implications of the absence of visioning. Without a clear vision, huge investments in the name of e-governance may not really contribute to improve the quality of life of citizens despite huge potential.

In order to improve the situation, it was thought to leverage information technology (IT) as a tool and fill the gap between the private primary schools and municipal schools. The vision was to bridge the gap of knowledge through digital learning aids.

Concept evolution

Considering the social disparities leading to difference in quality input of education, UNICEF came forward to adopt 30 municipal schools for computer-aided education. It was decided to use more graphics as medium of teaching and first train the teachers for presenting the lessons on computer. The idea was adopted from countries like Canada, Australia, etc., where they try to incorporate more visuals than lecture as a teaching aid.

Project implementation

Pilot project

UNICEF identified ILFS (Infrastructure Leasing and Financing Services)—a well known large corporate public limited company—to train the teachers in developing course contents with the digital aids and equipment. The course contents were developed through Power Point, Multi Media, Flash, etc. Initially, the pilot project started in a small way as mentioned below:

- UNICEF funded a pilot project covering 20 AMC schools with total 232 teachers. The time duration was six months and 10 days per batch were given.
- 116 teachers from 10 AMC schools were trained for one year through Outlook Gujarat Fund.
- The Education Training Services Unit of ILES provided faculties for further inputs for one year.

The teachers were quite enthusiastic and took lot of interest in the classroom. Thus, course contents were developed for 1st to 7th standard students. At the end of one year, the performances of these 30 schools were extremely good comparing to other municipal schools. The confidence-building of students and teachers from schools under the project was enormously high. The visual learning and teaching techniques also improved the teacher-student relationship. Further, the increased level of interactions improved the quality of education and better understanding of course contents by teachers as well as students. Attendance of the school children also increased. Because of these visible positive outcomes within a year, it was thought to implement computer-aided teaching techniques to all 563 municipal primary schools. Now, the scale was quite wide that needed strategic planning.

There were two main components of the project, running parallel to each other:

- developing the course contents and,
- training the teachers for the new system and make them computer literate.

The task of training the teachers was not only challenging but also necessary for further development of the project. Knowing this fact, the then Municipal Commissioner facilitated a series of interactions amongst all concerned towards training of all AMC school teachers.

Developing the course contents

The experience gained from the pilot project in 30 schools was useful to identify subject-wise training needs of the teachers. Based on that, different laboratories were set up to develop subject-wise course contents. In case of subjects like mathematics and science, additional laboratories were provided for different standards.

A total of 40 laboratories were opened as a developing centre in different locations. The locations were identified in such a way that the teachers can easily go to the laboratory at any time they feel like. Since the project warranted voluntary behaviour towards quality improvement, flexi-time pattern was adopted in these laboratories. The laboratories were equipped with latest PCs and LAN system. Every laboratory had:

- a technical coordinator who looks after technical equipments and the operational needs, and
- subject team that coordinates the course contents development for specific standard.

The team identifies the training needs and then development of the course contents was built on the basis of self-learning principles. Initially, this process took longer time but once the mindset was made, further development was much faster because of the high level of enthusiasm on ownership of the project. Teachers were encouraged to give innovative and creative ideas, which generated many interesting ways of teaching the same lesson.

Teachers' training programme

ILFS-ETS (Infrastructure Leasing and Financing Services–Education Training Services) played the role of a consultant for the training programme catering to all subject teachers from class 1 to 7. Initial trainings were founded on making the teachers familiar with the computers and related technologies. This helped building confidence of the teachers who were using the computers for the first time in their life.

- The training programme was structured for 20 days and 6 hours per day, which was divided into two phases of 10 days, each from 8 am to 2 pm.
- 26 Computer Resource Centres were set up in five zones as under:

  East Zone - 5 centres
  West Zone - 5 centres
  North Zone - 5 centres
  South Zone - 5 Centres
  Central Zone - 6 Centres

Figure 7.1
Distribution of course content

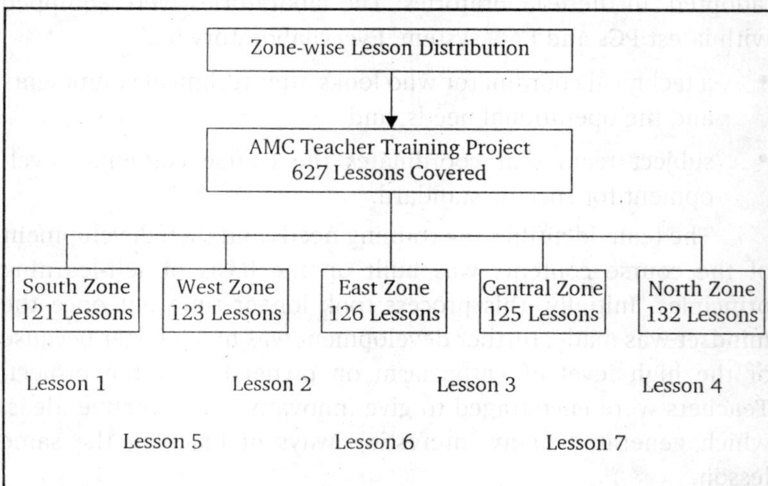

Figure 7.2
Zonal laboratories for course content development

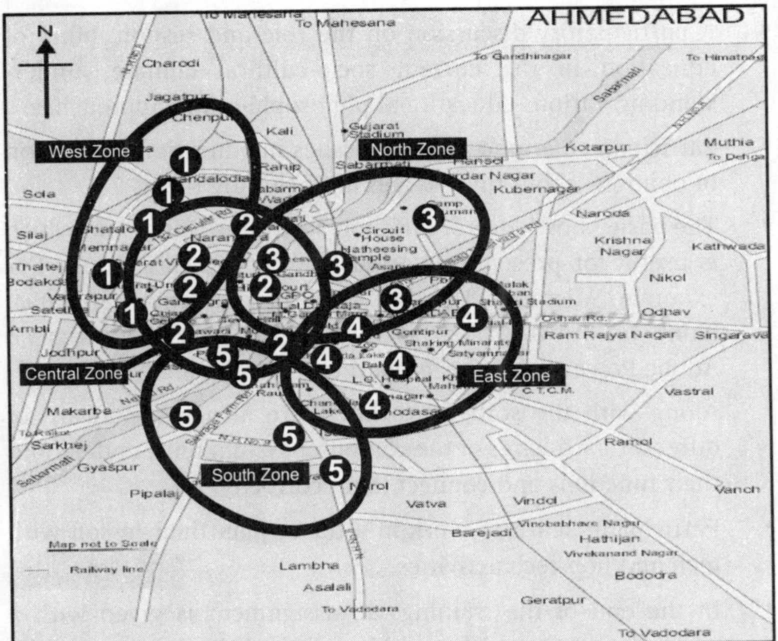

Total 26 Labs

❶ West Zone ❷ Central Zone ❸ North Zone ❹ East Zone ❺ South Zone

- Each batch comprised of 20 to 22 participants on an average
- A total of 9,328 participants were trained.
- A total of 505 batches were conducted, covering 563 AMC schools.

Phase I

The participants were made aware of the contents and sequencing of the training schedule. It includes:

- An overview of schoolnet (ILFS-ETC).

- This was followed by a brief explanation and recognition of different parts of the computer, introduction to desktop icons and keyboard etc.
- A participatory discussion on the role and responsibility of education in the current socio-cultural climate; understanding various educational philosophies and approaches.
- Participants became aware of issues in education, formation of opinions about these issues after sharing them.
- The basic knowledge of different softwares was given, which is useful for presenting various subjects in classrooms. For example, Microsoft Word, Excel (for mathematical data), Paint (for drawing objects), Internet (for easy connectivity), Adobe Power Point (for preparing lessons) etc.
- Along with the softwares, they were also made aware of different hardwares of the computer system unit; understand their functions and connect them correctly.
- Participants learn to work in a team, plan their lesson with tech and non-tech activities.
- In the end of the training, an assignment is given with a particular topic, which could be a little difficult to explain by the regular chalk and talk method. They utilize all the skills learnt during the course and create an interactive technology rich lesson out of it.
- Final presentation of the project work helped them in better understanding of abstract concepts.

Feedback from the ground

- Teachers feel motivated and want to acquire more skills.
- This has brought about an overall improvement in the enthusiasm level of students in better understanding the abstract concepts.
- They have become good listeners and are showing interest in learning when taught using the audio-video aids.

Phase II

- The primary objective was to enhance the skills learnt in phase I and create a rich tutorial containing lesson bank across standard 1-7 in all subjects.
- The lesson making had been planned so as to cover all the hard spots across all subjects for classes 1-7.
- A detailed interactive discussion had also been weaved in on the different learning styles of children based on the theory of 'Multiple Intelligence' by Sir Howard Gardner.
- The lesson plans were then prepared based on this concept.
- Discussion on softer skills of a teacher and classroom management issues had also been covered in this module.
- A specially designed offline e-mail package was developed to show how e-mail facility could be used. An off-line Internet surfing package was also developed.
- An off-line e-mail package was created since AMC labs do not have access to the net. Web browsing was also done offline with the help of stored sites.

Table 7.1
Lessons created from standard 1 to 7

	Gujarati	*Hindi*	*English*	*SS*	*Science*	*Maths*	*Sanskrit*	*PT*	*Total*
Std 1	12	-	-	-	-	09	-	-	21
Std 2	12	-	-	-	-	11	-	-	23
Std 3	20	-	-	-	15	12	-	-	47
Std 4	20	-	-	-	21	22	-	-	63
Std 5	28	18	18	33	20	14	-	14	145
Std 6	30	24	18	40	22	17	21	12	184
Std 7	29	25	20	38	20	17	17	18	184
Total	151	67	56	111	98	102	38	44	667

Training of trainers

This module was taken for 100 teachers selected from phase I and II, who in turn will act as Master Trainers with the knowledge of following:

Advanced MS Word

This was a bridge between the basic module and advance module and will act as a recap for those participants who have learnt this package earlier. The participants learnt about the advanced techniques of modifying the documents and can prepare presentable letters and reports. These skills could be used in making circulars, important documents, letters, mail merge in regional language etc.

Advanced MS Excel

Participants prepared a worksheet as per their work module in their firm using the utilities. They prepared a sheet with 'If-then-Else' formula to obtain conditional results and filter them as per requirement. They also generated sorted reports for the class, activities and reports concerned to school activities.

File management

This was the activity used to manage the lesson files created by all teachers during phase II. Moreover, the trainers are able to manage to take the back-up and install desired software on their own.

Hardware management

Trainers were taught the basic techniques to handle the computer more efficiently and technical knowledge to attach all the physical components of computer. Moreover, they learned how to take technical care of printer. Participants also learned the steps to prevent virus attack in computer.

CD burning and zipping the files

Activity to handle multiple files in a ZIP form and extracting it when and were desired through Win Zip and copying/burning the data on CD.

Figure 7.3
Teachers training and implementation in progress

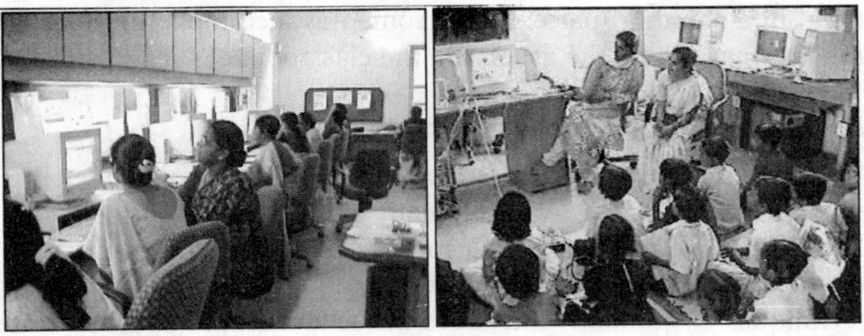

Figure 7.4
Teaching in progress

Figure 7.5
A lesson prepared by a student

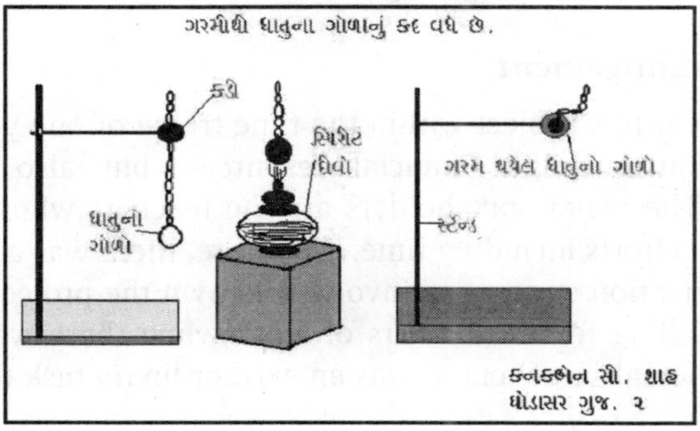

Advanced Power Point

Editing the lessons created in previous phases and modifying them in a standard pattern with some advance tools. Presenting the lessons with all the aspects in the classroom.

Economy of schoolnet project

To cover 2.25 lakh children spread out in 563 schools under the schoolnet programme was originally thought as a difficult job. The challenge faced was either totally replace the current pattern of teaching technique with computer-aided visual teaching techniques or gradually introduce the schoolnet programme over a period of 5-10 years. It was a very difficult task considering the expenditure involved. The main objective of introducing computer-aided teaching techniques was to improve the quality of education in the municipal schools and bridge the gap between private primary school children and municipal school children. Considering this, there was no room for implementing the project gradually over a period of ten years. Therefore, it was thought to mobilize all the resources and introduce it in all schools at the same time. The municipal administration was consulted and convinced that this project can be implemented within one year in all schools if in-house preparations are undertaken than outsourcing it. This could also bring down the fund requirement to not more than Rs. 4 crore. To overcome the initial resource constraints, mobile TV sets network with the single server was used in the schools to teach the children.

Problems faced during implementation

Change management

To implement this project within the time frame of one year, not only it requires huge financial resources, but also human resources. The major stakeholders are the teachers who have to put in extra efforts including time. Therefore, there was a need of special motivation strategy to involve and own the project by the teachers. Calling for extra hours of work when there was more number of female teachers, it was an extraordinary task to retain their motivation level for long duration till implementation of the project.

The pilot project in 30 municipal schools by UNICEF served well as a model and made the task little easier. Teachers and students from these schools were voluntarily sacrificing their summer vacations with a view to prepare the course contents for the next session. The other school teachers were brought to watch the happenings in these 30 schools which did have a "touch and feel" effect in achieving the success. It greatly helped to motivate the teachers to accept their responsibility and forgo the summer vacations to prepare the course contents for their students. Again, the in-house preparation activities met the teachers feel satisfied and motivated them to own the projects. The innovative thinking and creative ideas from the teacher community slowly filtered down to the students and generated greater enthusiasm and creative ideas in developing course contents and achieving the difference.

Resource crunch

The fund for implementing the project in all 563 schools was quite meagre and it was decided to prepare the lessons in-house for the same reason. Priority-wise, the resources were allocated first to meet the need of the laboratory equipment and training needs and then to individual classrooms.

Earlier, the course contents developed from the laboratories were periodically transferred to the school at random and then teachers were also allowed to make correction into it. Later, when lab-to-school activities increased, it was felt that every schoolroom required a visual display and it was difficult to meet such sudden demand because of resource crunch.

To meet the demand, the time-table was rearranged in such a way that two TV sets on wheel carrier were provided to each school and moved into different classrooms as per the subject need. Selection of the subjects was also prioritized and the language subjects were initially omitted from the project scope.

Later, the municipal councillors were requested to utilize their development fund to buy computer and TV/projection screens for the municipal primary schools.

Results

- All municipal schools got computers installed with other learning equipments.
- Most of the teachers got familiarized with computers and prepared course contents through Power Point.
- School children from the slum areas could get familiarize with computers and computer-aided learning.
- Quality of education from the municipal schools could improve substantially and can be now compared with private schools.
- School children from the poor segments of the society could build the gap of digital divide.
- Overall positively changed computer-aided learning environment could generate high involvement of students in developing course contents.
- Better quality education effectively reduces school dropout rate and prevent dropped out children to getting into criminal activities.
- Higher percentage of promotion to higher classes.

Conclusion

Despite finding resources for such project was very difficult, the elected body appreciated the method in which it was implemented. Within a year it could be seen that the overall quality of educational input has increased. The children could understand the lessons easily and preferred to attend the school thus reducing dropout rate in primary schools. It created more awareness and enthusiasm in students as well as teachers. The changed atmosphere made more students to participate in developing course contents.

The major issue is sustenance of the project with regular upgradation of course contents. The project of this kind has lot of intangible benefits. The continued budgetary support for the maintenance of computer laboratories and connectivity needs assurance from AMC administration.

8

Change Management

The concept of change management has been discussed in the introductory chapter of this book. Change management is a common theme, which was relevant while implementing all the case study projects. That is the reason, why it is important to discuss how the process of change management was actually made applicable in Gujarat state transport department and Ahmedabad city administration, using information technology (IT) as primary tool for e-governance. It can be viewed from two different angles based on the way it was implemented: one, at state level, related to transport department and the other at city administration level, concerning various departments. The latter was more difficult as it directly involved large number of employees and citizens. A database was created to integrate tax and service information system, engineering information system, health information system and employee information system where all citizens can interact with the administration. The scope of the application included monetary and non-monetary transactions pertaining to citizen forums, citizen complaints and their redressal, public health and sanitation, infrastructure development, online tenders, business licences and other registrations, building plan approval system, registration of births and deaths, all revenue collections etc. The task of changing the process of citizens' interaction with the administration from birth to death was quite exhaustive one, which is discussed in this chapter through the successful example of Ahmedabad Municipal Corporation (AMC).

Key challenges for change management campaign

Like commercial marketing, change management or social marketing offers a logical planning process involving consumer-oriented research, marketing analysis, market segmentation, objective setting and the identification of strategies and tactics. It is based on the voluntary exchange of costs and benefits between two or more parties. However, change management is more difficult than commercial marketing. It involves changing intractable behaviours in complex organizations like state transport department and AMC. Moreover, marketing for changing conventional management system to e-governance system is even more complex, as demand has to be created for the idea or product concept. Here, the citizens as customers should demand faster services through IT tools. In the absence of collective forum to create such demand conventional paper-based system would be seen as better by the citizens than to experiment new system.

The processes are more complex

Traditionally something tangible—a physical good can be exchanged with a price. But, when it extends beyond physical, different strategies are required for services. In change management, (i.e., implementation of e-governance in urban local government or in licencing department), the product is the service delivery which goes beyond physical. This complexity makes change management difficult.

Varied demand

As a change management champion, the Transport Commissioner or Municipal Commissioner had not only to uncover new demand, but in addition had to frequently deal with negative demand when the primary stakeholder, i.e., citizens are apathetic about or strongly resistant to a proposed system change. The stakeholders, for instance, may see no problems with the current system. In these situations, social marketers had to challenge entrenched attitudes and beliefs.

Challenging target groups

The most obvious source of competition in change management is the stakeholder's tendency to continue in his or her current behavioural patterns. Inertia is a very powerful competitor.

Apart from that, there are also groups within stakeholders, which are least accessible and least likely to change their behaviour. They often constitute the powerful lobby and as their personal, social and practical resources may dry up, they are most unresponsive to interventions. Thus, vested interest groups, corrupt employees and popularity-oriented elected members or employee union leaders try to discourage target audiences.

Greater stakeholders' involvement required

Change management process divides the final outcome into high and low involvement categories, whereas management system reform deals with which the stakeholder is very highly involved (lifestyle changes). Thus, it generally is more difficult to get a stakeholder to agree.

·The implementation process

The change management implementation process involves following steps:

- Tools selected
- Strategy adapted
- Planning process to implement
- Issues addressed and solution found in the process

Tools used for change management

As stated earlier, taking the advantage of automation and technology innovation, a database was created to integrate tax and service information system, engineering information system, health information system and employee information system. The scope of the application includes the transactions (monetary and non-monetary) pertaining to the following functions:

- Licence and permit issuances and transparent regulations
- Tax assessments for motor vehicles
- Tax collections
- Citizen forums
- Citizens' complaints and their redressal
- Public health and sanitation
- Infrastructure development
- Online tenders
- Business licences and other registrations
- Building plan approval system
- Registration of births and deaths
- All revenue collections
- Property tax assessment and collections

Strategy

Mix strategy for marketing

In these case studies, the marketing mix strategies included the following elements:

- The 'product' could be any of these three behaviours: getting proper tax assessment, every year assessing tax for quarterly or annual payment and instant licence issuance.
- The 'price' of engaging in these behaviours includes the monetary costs of the tax assessment by visits, motor vehicle inspection, the property and survey, potential discomfort and/or embarrassment.
- The 'places' that these services are offered are in the six city civic centres located in different parts of the city, banks, Internet, depending upon the needs of the target audience or

inter-state border RTO check-posts or RTO offices where licences are issued.

- 'Promotion' was done through public service announcements, billboards, media events and community outreach.
- The 'public' addressed include all the stakeholders such as employees, citizens, transporters and elected members and those who influence their decisions like the physicians, policy makers, advocates, teachers, etc.
- 'Partnerships' could be cultivated between all the three stakeholders, viz., employees, citizens and elected members.
- The 'policy' aspect of the campaign was focused on citizens' rights, easy accessibility to information, quick delivery of services, empowerment, stress-free working environment, great level of reduction of opportunities for bad practices or corruption and transparent procedures etc.
- The 'purse strings' were from the state government of Gujarat and also from AMC budget.

Each of the above elements of the marketing mix strategy was taken into consideration when the programmes were under development, for that was the core of the marketing effort. Marketing research was used to elucidate and shape the final product, price, place, promotion and other related decisions.

Strategy for stakeholder orientation

Besides using information technology as basic tool to achieve the objectives, both the Transport Department and the AMC understood that internal marketing should be the major tool to bring in these attitudinal changes in the stakeholders. Good governance in urban corporate body was planned to bring in by an effective replacement of conventional paper-based system with e-governance system. Since the stakeholders involved were in millions, and the employees were in tens of thousands, motivation tools were planned to be training, mass communication, frequent and accessible informal communication channel between the

Figure 8.1

Role of change management in the process

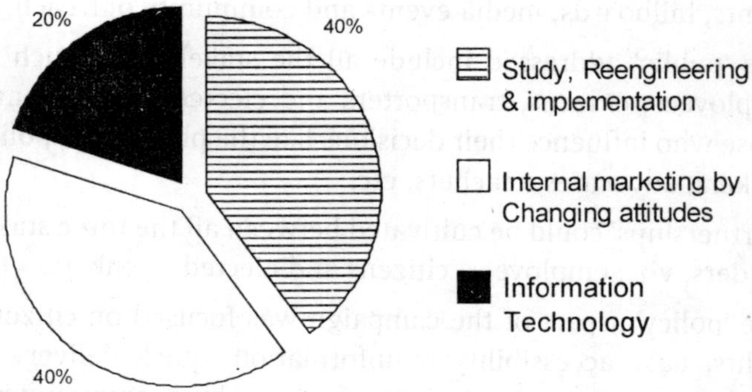

stakeholders and the Commissioners of Transport Department and AMC.

When a replacement of total system is involved there is a need to analyze change management framework. Such change management framework requires 40 percent of internal marketing by changing attitudes of stakeholders, another 40 percent of systems' study and re-engineering process and 20 percent of IT (Figure 8.1).

Regular focus on motivating the team members

According to the proportionate contribution of activities as described in Figure 8.1, the strategies were drawn. Major emphases were given to employees' motivation to accept the changes. This activity needed extensive training programmes and well-established and accessible informal communication channel between the chief of the organization and the employees. The employees with adequate experience and who would accept challenge and change were identified. They took the leadership in forming the core task team to develop new systems. Two months, intensive training to these task teams and informal communication channel created a friendly environment and motivated them slowly to suggest how to reduce steps involved in manual operations to a very few steps if computer automation is to be brought in. The list of steps for different activities was called as 'flow chart'. Special celebrations were organized to mark the innovation of flow charts as if it was a major breakthrough in software design and in implementation of e-governance system. This motivated the task team members to own the project.

The team then drew more members for each activity to recheck the flow charts and to monitor the writing of software programmes. Professional programmers in the presence of the task team members of each activity wrote software from the flow charts. Witnessing their flow chart converted into software had magical effect on the task team members in owning the project. This was the milestone of the project implementation. The steps were adapted in both Transport Department and AMC.

In AMC elected council members were also informed from time to time in every General Board meeting that the e-governance project on implementation would make them popular as it would deliver civic services very fast and bring lot of revenue to carry out long pending civic works in their ward. Except a few, almost all welcomed such steps.

Print and visual media were used every week announcing the development in change over of new system. Citizens were informed from time to time also about what kind of services are going to be offered in the new civic centres and through e-governance system.

Planning process

All task team members were involved in creating system approach and integration of these applications (activity) software. Being involved in every step of creation of a large volume of database-based e-governance project, the task team members kept informally communicating their achievements to other colleagues and invited them to see how it works. This activity convinced a large number of employees that their workload would tremendously reduce once the new system comes. Considering the swing in favour of e-governance changes, it was planned to totally replace the old system with new automation. This outright decision was taken as a strategy that it is better to face the new problems (bugs in software) than to have a parallel manual procedures operating along with e-governance system. This was a key decision as some studies reveal that most of the e-governance projects in the world failed because of a trial (pilot) e-governance system experimented along with conventional manual procedures and those employees used to conventional manual procedures create an environment to completely discourage automation. The total replacement of every activity with new e-governance system was introduced one by one successfully in AMC by the task team members along with other employees. Debugging procedures carried out on site in the employees' presence made them to believe that the new systems are workable. The process flows of activities were as follow:

- Every activity was separately dealt by a task team, consisting of different levels of employees from the relevant activity department and a technical expert from the implementing agency.
- Task team regularly met to assess the progress and to share how their co-employees perceive the development in their workplace.
- Steps removed or added in activity delivering process had lot of informal pooling of suggestions from the co-employees.
- Reduced level of steps of activity through computerization also were shared by the employees, this helped that they knew what is going to come.
- Prior to writing programme all the employees of the concerned departments were informed.
- This process of sharing of information created a smooth environment to change over from manual to computer delivery systems.

Achieved change management: Step by step

There can be many areas where the change management can be applied. Following are some achievements in case of Transport Department and AMC since the beginning of e-governance to the progress till date:

Transport Department

1. *Smart card driving licence:* 1 kb memory chip-based driving licence with biometric identification forced every licence applicant to personally visit the RTO office and obtain the licence instantly after the driving test. This removed the earlier practice of engaging illegal agents to get the driving licence who thrived on indulging in bad practices.
2. *Inter-state border check-posts:* Fully automated and computerized inter-state border RTO check-posts could enable 100 percent checking of vehicles and cleared every vehicle in one or two minutes. This removed the uncertainty of tax arrears or overloading penalty from the transporters' point of view. Despite the penalty rates per tonnage were reduced the revenue increased manifold and the harassment faced by transporters were eliminated.
3. *Smart optical card registration certificate book for motor vehicles:* A hybrid form of 1 kb memory chip and 1.5 mb optical strip with system enabled unique PIN (personal identification number) replaced the paper-based RC book which prone to forgery and tax evasion. This eliminated harassment to the honest tax payers and arrested the tax evasion thus increasing legitimate government revenue.
4. *MIS:* By providing 64 kbps networking connectivity with all field offices and check-posts with the central monitoring centre, lengthy paper correspondences were eliminated and vehicles were not detained. On the spot tax verification and tax collection removed harassment meted out to the motor vehicle owners and increased government revenue. Further, every transaction in the department is recorded and stored for future processes.

Ahmedabad Municipal Corporation

1. *Financial transactions:* To have demonstrative effect on all stakeholders, the applications like all pay-in and pay-out activities were transferred to ICICI Bank (second largest bank in India and rated as one of the best bank in Asia) through a secured network so as to avail finance and accounts expertise from the bank. Primary consideration was to eliminate corruption in manual pay-out system. As a result, highly corrupt prone accounts department was replaced by an automatic system networked with ICICI Bank.
2. *Building plan permissions:* Similarly, issuing building plan permissions, which normally takes anywhere between six months to two years, were put in automation on predefined parameters and now permissions are issued instantly through the system with electronic signatures. These instant approvals had immense effect on citizens and employees. Citizens' evoked interest in sustaining such quick services and employees otherwise had no alternative except to accept to these changes.
3. *City civic centre:* Continued informal communication with task team and employees made them own the projects. Employees only were trained to operate the civic centre counters delivering services to citizens. Continued feedback and upgradation of the system to more user-friendly created on pressure-free working environment. Civic centres located in gardens created a pleasant feeling to citizens. Instant issuance of licences, certificates, complaint redressal made citizens feel pleasant against their earlier experience in standing in long queues for hours under hot sun without even having drinking water and toilet facilities.
4. *Property tax assessment:* Tax assessment on property used to be a highly disputed activity of AMC employees. Every year, 55,000 court cases were filed against one million properties of the city. High discretionary powers vested with tax assessor made them rich overnight. High resistances were faced from this group and employees and top and middle

level tax employees opposed the change vehemently. Quick action by replacing top and middle level tax staff with youngsters of the task team forced low level employees to accept the changes.

5. *E-learning schoolnet project:* Under the project, a number of computer laboratories to train teachers of, and develop course contents in, all the 563 municipal primary schools were created. About 2.25 lakh students from poor section of the society could improve their education quality and progress to better performance. School dropout rates reduced drastically because of better method of teaching.

Issues

Transport Department

Employees were the major stakeholders in departmental projects. They have to implement the transition which supposed to deprive their personal benefits. Transporters were major beneficiary because these projects eliminated the harassment and every transaction recordable. The internal information and experience sharing had been crucial to build the system design. The employee motivation and continuous information flow, from both top to bottom and bottom to top, helped to understand that it is better for all to change the system. Procurement decisions were taken by the government and hence external problems were not faced in implementing the projects.

Ahmedabad Municipal Corporation

A standing committee is a body headed by an elected member, which meets every week to take decisions on civic works. The decisions for placing work orders, procurement of machines and materials are made by elected members. On many occasions, the chairman of the committee, who is the main decision-maker, despite the advise of the Municipal Commissioner, may take decisions which may not be workable. Since the state government did the funding of e-governance project, the procurement procedures were carried out by a state government agency which made implementation possible. A few members with vested interest opposed the project and the system change. Since print and electronic media widely favoured the project and internal pressures were brought in by the mayor and a few members forced the standing committee to accept the project. A number of elected members were taken to see other successful e-governance projects as a measure to build pressure on the vested interests. Eventually, after three months of extensive public and media support, this anti-group could be prepared to support the project.

Finance

Transport Department

Because of the importance to increase the government's legitimate revenue, the project funding was completely done by the government including the land acquisition. Roads and bridges for the check-posts demanded large funding, which was met by the Roads and Buildings Department.

Ahmedabad Municipal Corporation

It was initially easy to convince the elected wing about the financing of the project since funding was from the state government. .However, in a elected urban local body, the procurement process attracted quite a vested interest from the elected wing. It was diverted by asking government-owned company (Gujarat Informatics Ltd.) to undertake the procurement process.

Security

Transport Department

Since tax assessment and collections were involved, system security was of prime importance. The system architecture was built in such a way that the inbuilt fire walls make the system fool-proof. While designing the architecture, it was presumed that some day someone would try to penetrate the system. This made us to think many possible ways to strengthen the system.

Ahmedabad Municipal Corporation

When the ICICI Bank agreed to connect the payment gateway, there was a serious worry about the secured connectivity. Many technical experts visited and explored various alternative possibilities. We thought someone would one day penetrate the system, hence we should be fully prepared. Network architecture was totally customized in such a way that it becomes impossible to penetrate by changing language in different servers and installed encrypted four code programmes. Even when the worms hit the whole world in November 2003, this system functioned safely.

Daily update of data

Transport Department

The networking connectivity with all field offices with the central monitoring centre enabled the system to update the data at regular intervals. Off-line checking of driving licences and vehicle permits was designed in such a way that data updations are carried out automatically once in twenty-four hours.

Ahmedabad Municipal Corporation

In a municipal administration daily updating of data is a cumbersome task since it never had been like this. Tax arrears keep mounting but the manual system works on its own speed. Birth and death register having data of millions of persons was a herculean task to put in the database and provide enough mechanism to update it on daily basis. Dedicated team of more than 100 persons continuously worked for more than ten months to enter and devise updation process.

Dependency on machines

Transport Department

The system was built on high dependency on machines. Sustainability was a question when the offices were located in remote places. Initial effective monitoring increased the revenue by manifold and the employees operating the system could not go back to reduced level of revenue which created a compulsion to maintain minimum operation. Cases had been noticed that there had been number of shut downs of the systems, particularly in the check-posts, however the revenue flow could not be reduced but optimal increase was at stake.

Ahmedabad Municipal Corporation

Most of the employees and elected members often raised the issue of dependency of machines. In case of any serious shut down the functions should not kept held up. To meet this situation, temporarily paper-based system also was maintained. Because of fool-proof system design, till now, there had been no occasion for such contingency.

Outcomes

- Elimination of harassment to tax payers and citizens.
- Effective implementation of licencing regulations.
- Transparent transactions.
- Transactions are recorded and stored.
- Strong and efficient organization with state-of-the-art system in place.
- Speedy and quality delivery of civic services to citizens.
- Efficient citizen complaints address and redressal system citizen forum for a citizen to participate in AMC activities.
- Instant issuance of building plan permission.
- Easy access to tax assessment information.
- Outline revenue collection.
- Reduced costs.

- Higher and sustainable revenue.
- Gain economic prosperity.
- Clean environment and improved health conditions.
- Improved customer service/satisfaction.
- Electronic processing built bridge on digital divide between common man and the government.

Table 8.1 shows the comparison between the working atmospheres before and after e-governance projects were implemented.

Table 8.1
Social transition

Earlier (before September 18, 2002)	*Now*
In-line	Online
Dependency at each level	Independent
Discretionary powers, execution	All treated the same
Decentralized Database	Centralized database
People had to go to particular zone for tax payment or to lodge complaints	City civic centres, banks, Internet and credit card
Manual interest calculation	Real-time interest calculation
Information available on paper	Information available on net
Information within the hold of a few	Easily accessible for the citizen
Lengthy and fault prone procedure	Simple and speedy
MIS was non existent	MIS online
Go to different departments and places for tax and fees payment	City civic centres or Internet and one-stop at RTO check-posts
Suffocated atmosphere for citizen/employee	User-friendly vibrant atmosphere
Lack of connectivity – inadequate deployment of resources	Optimum use of resources
No accountability	Online employee performance
Citizen became vested interest	Trust citizen-citizen centric system
All manual activities and billing etc.	Computer does all the task

A special note is that the AMC e-governance website got about 3,51,000 hits within a year because Gujarat having commercially enterprising community hold properties in the city of Ahmedabad but spread out all over the world for business. They extensively used the AMC web to seek information and pay taxes. The comparable revenue collection of last year to this year from April to October has gone up from Rs. 200 million to Rs. 1,100 million.

SWOT analysis: Promises and limits of the project

Strength

- Largest centralized online city government database.
- Updated round the clock.
- Total transparency of the government activities to the common citizen in any government department.
- First biometric identification introduced in smart card driving licence.
- First artificial intelligence used in India for e-governance application in RTO inter-state border check-posts by using licence plate recognition system.
- AMC is the only municipal corporation in India to provide total e-governance solution.
- AMC is the only municipal corporation in India to provide building plan approval online.
- Replication is possible elsewhere in the world with appropriate change management techniques.

Weakness: Branding in the non-profit environment

- *Sustenance needs continuous technological upgradation*: For many non-profit organizations, one of the most confounding aspects of marketing is the matter of branding. But powerful causes deserve powerful brands. Branding of such e-governance project covering millions should influence the entire organization, prompting employees and citizens alike to constantly reinforce and burnish the Gujarat government's Transport Department and AMC's essence and identity. It has many impacts on resource sharing, kind of employees and talent comes to work for the cause etc. Government organizations may typically lack brand focus, which should be reflected at every touch point with customers, not just external contacts and communications. Unfortunately, it is difficult to enforce brand discipline among governmental organizations because there are no repercussions for non-implementation of such projects. Perhaps most important is that branding is a new idea for most non-profit and governmental organizations.

- *Cost of adoption*: The total cost of adopting this change management or practice often goes beyond the monetary price alone as further cost-related factors are typically involved including the time lost or spent together with perceived barriers to adoption—be they psychological, social, or physical. Reducing such costs and creating incentives to adopt and maintain the new idea thus increase further value.

Opportunity: Future benefits of change management

These are typical case studies driving the point that "it is not the technology is important, but the man behind the technology is more important". Technologies did exist prior to the projects, but it is a case where a champion could mobilize the resources to motivate the stakeholders to accept and own the changes through change management techniques. The informal communication channel, intensive training and other change management techniques had been the major reason for successful implementation of this project. Internal marketing and relationship management played key role to change the attitudes of all the stakeholders that enabled the organization to break the vicious circle existed between the stakeholders. Such change management processes may set the future trend in the direction of major social changes in various sectors by leveraging IT as e-governance tool.

Threat: Vested employees and other interests

When a large number of employees are involved in a large volume of transactions, the vested interests would always play the role to destroy any system, which comes on their way. For example, building plan approval is an activity wherein the user and the regulator jointly connive and find easy solutions to beat the system. Opposition to automat this approval on predetermined parameters was enormous. Even after implementing it sustaining was another problem. However determined team work could see to it that those vested interests had limited space to play.

Conclusion

Change is a difficult aspect to accept. Bringing change is still more difficult. Enforcing complete replacement of a system, which erodes the power overnight from the dominant groups was not an easy task. A determined team could see to that system could be changed and could be sustained. Strategies planned to involve all stakeholders formally and informally helped. Speed and avoidance of delay had been the mantra because many believed that this project would not come through because of number of employees and elected members involved.

9

Lessons

The aims of e-governance are to provide greater access to information, to promote participation in the decision-making process by creating more opportunities for people to interact, to increase transparency that can result in increased public sector accountability and reduced opportunities for corruption and to achieve efficiency through cost and time savings. The success of the projects in achieving any or all of the above objectives would largely depend on three factors. First relates to choice of the problem area for e-application. A problem that is likely to yield maximum impact would be the right project to undertake. If the impacts (monetary or otherwise) were significant, then there would be sufficient pressure to force the decision-makers to keep the system function well. Technology need not be a limiting factor in any of these decisions. Secondly, participation of all the stakeholders from the beginning in a full-fledged manner is necessary for the project to reach its operation stage and sustain in the long term. Finally, the commitment of the initiator and quick decision process would enable realization of the project and its benefits. These factors are critical for success as e-governance does involve substantial use of information technology (IT) applications, which is a fast changing field.

Many opinions and views exist about e-governance system development and its sustenance. The most common of all is to think that e-governance can simply be materialized by purchasing more computers and putting up a website or by automating administrative practices. This is not true because technological innovations will not change the mentality of bureaucrats who do not perceive the citizens as customers of government and realize their potential as participants in government decision-making process. It has to be well understood that computerizing complex procedures or purchasing more advanced technology cannot bring effectiveness in governance.

This chapter attempts to provide some strategic inputs based on all the case study examples that may be of use to e-governance practitioners. It has been organized in three major parts: the first part deals with problems of project implementation that are more technical in nature, whereas the second one identifies factors that are critical for success and the final part concludes.

Project development and implementation issues

The learning from the case studies suggests that the process of implementing e-governance can be divided into four phases. These can also be viewed as different components of the whole system. They are system development, system configuration, networking and management of database. Though all of them are independent of each other, the implementation framework is not complete without their integration.

System development

The system development decisions range from policy issues related to project selection to project design.

Focus on 'governance problem'

In case of e-governance initiatives a clear statement of vision, policies and strategies at the national/state level or for sectors is generally absent. It would take a long time to prepare such policy perspective. On the other hand, the opportunities are dynamic and the technology is changing rapidly. Therefore, the champions without waiting for higher-level policies have to address organizational concerns, recognize the latest IT developments and evolve the system design. Many times it also happens that quite a projects are first-time projects. So, it is desired that clear understanding of the paper system and its pitfalls are identified. Based on this a strategic plan needs to be evolved. Once this is finalized, it can be shared appropriately to gain political, peer group and other stakeholders' acceptance.

While selecting a project, it is to be noted that e-governance is a tool to move towards good governance. One is not interested in developing e-projects to prove one's technological advancements. The process is important, by which core governance problems are resolved. Hence, projects in the field of e-governance should have a goal that supports the overall objectives of good governance. This means that the project search for implementation would have to begin by identifying the 'core' governance issues rather than focus on easy implementation prospectus. Of the several core issues, choose a segment, which is large enough to make visible impact. For example, in case of Transport Department, the core problem was revenue leakage due to corrupt practices. Once the problem area was identified rightly, technology search and application development took place. Subsequently, e-application was extended to simpler but less impacting areas as a matter of routine.

In sum, it may be said that *problem focused* and *not ease of application* should be the criteria to decide the choice of the project.

Laying out the system for service delivery

With the focus on solving the core governance problem, one should identify the main problem and its associated problems in terms of their significance and the sources. The problems like redundancies and delay, scope for manipulation, etc., have to be explicitly drawn up through process flow charts. This will help in analyzing the problem and detail out the objectives. Then, alternative methods of delivery have to be evaluated against indicators developed to assess the achievement in project objectives. This systematic process will help to avoid the policy of hardware first and instal any software available in the market practice. Instead, it will be possible to figure out the correct technology alternative and avoid future confusions.

In complex situations, it is often recommended to carry out pilot project and then further implementation is carried out. If the pilot project is successful, the implementation will be expanded and if not, make another pilot project or cancel implementation. There are many successful projects and there is similarity also with many inter-departmental applications. However, there is no case in India where a successful project is replicated except smart card driving licence system. Reasons can be many but this author is of the view that pilot projects are operated under 'special' circumstances and each circumstance is different, so there is very little scope for replication.

There is also a common belief that a step-by-step approach starting with 'information sharing', then 'interaction', subsequently to 'transaction' and finally reaching to 'transformation' is preferable. While this appears systematic, application of 'e' becomes more important here and not the core governance problem, which should dictate the process. Ultimately, it may happen that through this phasing process, one may never reach the final goal within the reasonable time frame. Therefore, as stated earlier, "application of 'e' solution to the core problem area" is a preferred approach.

Systems approach

The trend in IT system design is towards separate application processing from a common database that is used to support it. The common database is a mechanism by which data items are integrated across many applications and made consistently available to a variety of users. For efficient functioning, it is better that the information system is designed as a planned federation of small systems. But, an overall information system plan should be made to guide the integration of diverse information system application. Even though, application systems are implemented at a time, the overall plan can determine how they fit in with other functions.

Overall system integration deserves greater emphasis on methodical planning: detailing the work practices, inter-organizational coordination and fast adaptability for technological changes. Citizen-oriented organizations contribute to the evolutions of ever more complex information and communication systems. In such environment, the rational planning becomes difficult because of fast structural changes in the economic and political environments. However, for long-term planning and to make provision for accommodating fast changes in technology, it is better to formulate a team of steering group to monitor the events and changes happening in IT.

Foreseeing future evaluation of inter-departmental functions and enhancing the IT infrastructure for such events does not realize at the initial formation of e-governance projects affecting only one particular department. Government to business (G2B) e-government projects and government to citizen (G2C) e-governance projects have wide gap of applications. G2C e-governance projects are likely to evolve at a faster pace, which can have impact on other applications also. Visualizing and estimating time for such occurrences need high priority and greater importance even if it has a cost. Perhaps, this cost can be accommodated in future projects. It is not necessary that a uniform design is applicable to all state governments and departments. However, at the design stage itself, the system can be enabled with futuristic features in database design, hardware and software specifications. Thus, a holistic approach would definitely pay dividend at a later stage and would improve the efficiency of the organization.

System configuration

Once the project plan is ready, the next phase is to configure the operational components and their specifications that are necessary to run the system. Decisions about system configuration depend upon the expected output from the proposed activity, available budget and technology. It includes assessment of data volume, activities, process, service delivery, data updating frequency, storage capacity and to foresee future needs.

Configuration management

Configuration management itself is a discipline, which keeps watch on all the stages of development and maintenance. Software configuration is key to the software process as it includes many activities that must be carried out simultaneously and consistently. Moreover, it involves many different individuals such as users, managers, software engineers and hardware engineers.

Configuration management systems design: Some organizations give control to support groups that have expertise in a particular technology or platform, because it may not be cost-effective to train central staff in specialist areas. In these cases, the support group manager is responsible for the control of configuration integration owned and maintained by the group. The organization's procedures for change management, configuration management, release management and a centralized configuration management database should be adopted wherever possible.

These may be defined in a change and configuration management plan for the organization and be supported by functional and design documents for the configuration management system. The relationships between the plans should be documented to help staff to see the context of configuration management within their group, with the manager of each group signing off its plan. Lower-level plans should align with, and refer up to the higher-level plans so as to avoid duplication.

Software configuration management: The software configuration management needs the following coordinating functions:

- *Configuration identification*: The type of software components that will be under control, their baselines and how they will work.
- *Configuration control*: The technical and administrative procedures in order to control the changes in the components.
- *Configuration audit*: The function that seeks the current status of any software component.
- *Configuration status accounting*: The function that provides the development history of any software component by recording the actions of the above function.

In addition to the above definitions, three more functions, which deserve attentions, are:

- *Manufacture*: The function that manages the construction and building of the software product in an optimal manner.
- *Process management*: Ensures the proper implementation of the organization procedures, policies, and lifecycle model.
- *Team work*: The function that controls the work and interactions between multiple developers.

Data transactions: Eventually, the system configuration activities are interdependent including communication network. The volume of data transaction happens across geographically distant locations and from multiple users. Loss or erosion of data may occur if the networking is not adequately designed. Considering global positioning systems and global indexing systems, transactions of graphic data are going to dominate and in that case the volume of data transactions even with lesser resolutions is likely to be many times higher than that of digital data transactions. Therefore, at the configuring stage, it is always better to plan with futuristic options.

Network configuration: There had been cases where at the initial stage of application installations and limited modular functions, the organizations go for 64 kbps leased lines for communication network considering the high cost of the V-Sat connectivity compared to lesser data volume transactions. Half the way through a need may arise compulsorily to go for V-Sat communications with the bandwidth of 2 mbps or even more. If so, then the investment on the leased lines may go waste. Additional investment and additional time requirement can be saved if, at the planning stage itself, the network configuration is given adequate cushion and accordingly the decision is taken.

As systems can become obsolete fast, there is no specific design for providing accommodation to the flexibility that may occur. However, sudden paradigm shift can collapse the whole function. The state governments or team of departments can evolve system configurations for three sets of data processing factors:

1. Static factors
2. Variable factors
3. Influencing factors

Other area of consideration is that the components undergo significant rate of change. Software, especially the large-scale systems are bound to undergo numerous conflicting changes during their lifetime. Versions have unique identifiers. A version identifier is a double identification with variation identifier and revision identifier. Variations represent independent lines of development and each consists of an ordered sequence of revision. Revisions result from changes, the purpose of which is to fix bugs. Each variation has a set of attributes that are of primary interest to the system designers.

Development and evolution process

Although there is an obvious relationship between the software development process and the processes of software evolution, the two are most often loosely coupled. Both processes include an ordered set of steps that are controlled by the managers of the software project. The development steps are of many different types depending on the lifecycle model size of the software project and l e tools used in development.

Evolutionary change of systems: Cost on obsolete replacement and plan space for updating evolutionary change of systems depends on the size of the organizations and data warehouse. In smaller organizations, it is easier to replace the obsolete systems instead of investing on unforeseen evolutionary changes at the design stage itself whereas large organizations or large size of data need to have high security with planned space for evolutionary changes in the system. In large organizations like government, most of the functions are well defined and sudden changes are rare. So, it provides enough opportunity to plan software evolution during system configuration itself.

Hardware and software integration

Most of the government employees believe that once the front-end screen is ready, it means that total computerization of the department is ready for operation. They are not aware that the system would not work without the backend support and network. Therefore, more often, IT gurus advocate for in-house system design and development to familiarize the employees, which is essential in creating a sense of ownership of the project.

The data warehousing can primarily provide categorical structure for static data and variable data. Any addition of variable data to certain static data would enable automatic conversion of the static data to influencing data. Data structure further would enable automatic modification of relevant database. The variable factors can be periodic and perhaps relational to many coefficient factors of the database. Consideration of such dynamic nature of data at the designing stage may be very difficult to categorize and structure but can save the system from becoming obsolete and provide space in simpler model to system configuration.

In a fast-changing technology, the IT managers worldwide are being confronted with the question how to configure the hardware. Hardware of a system today becomes obsolete tomorrow. 'Speed' is the buzzword in "Network Access Technologies". Accessibility and accuracy are of prime importance to e-government systems. The system designer should bear twenty years ahead in mind while configuring the hardware.

Database management system

Aggregate volumes of data of one state government would run into extraordinarily large volume, which deserves special database management system. It is likely that most of the government departments process similar information for different functional activities. If every department stores such large information in the database, it would overload the database with lot of redundancies. Thus, optimal functions of the data warehousing need a design that should be for the whole state government instead of a particular department. Since decision support systems (DSS) from one governmental department to another vary, the processing pattern need to be designed at the design stage itself according to the functional requirement.

Every major company selling database management system (DBMS) products may advocate that their product is the most suitable for the government applications, unconcerned with the kind of architecture and data volume and the transaction patterns. It is the system manager who needs to define the architecture and the systems approach before implementing modular applications in governmental organizations. High security and zero erosion of data during storage and replication are the key issues that need to be categorically addressed while finalizing the vendor and technology for DBMS.

Data volume measurement methods

There is no simple method to assess the data volume. The static data and processing data may vary from one department to another and also from one period of time to another. The user need and the system design only can determine the data volume and the data transaction patterns for processing. Frequent additions on the load of the data volume and changes in the processing pattern may destabilize the DBMS. Ultimately, there is no single method to determine the method on which data volume can be assessed and structured to suit the functional need for all the departments. The database structure should have multi-dimensional processing pattern (Figure 9.1) tailored not

Figure 9.1

Three-dimensional configure model for e-governance

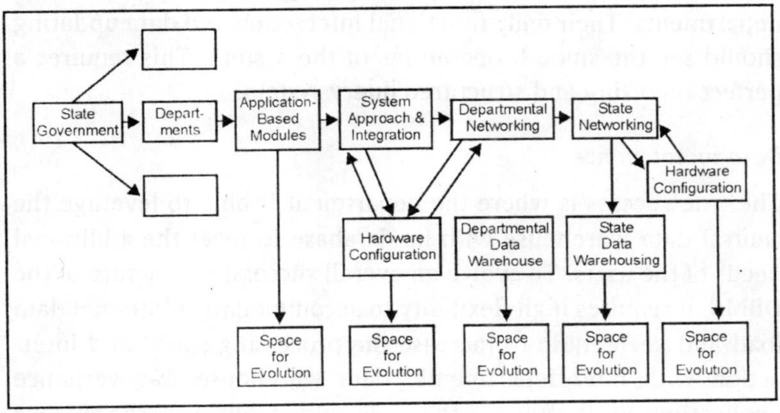

only to the need of the department but also the end users, i.e., the citizens.

Database architecture

There cannot be a common design for every state government. The design and structure depend on the total population, area and infrastructure availability and the interaction period with the citizens that can vary daily, weekly, monthly, quarterly or annually depending on functions of the department. Similarly, there cannot be a universal design for the departments within a state government. Availability of infrastructure in different geographical locations for the network is also a factor to determine the modular applications-based systems approach.

In a typical social welfare department, the benefit deliveries are in kinds and therefore the processing pattern may be totally different from other departments, which may promote tourism or collect tax etc. Processing patterns and network of regulatory department would be different from that of others. Under these complex functional environments, the database architecture needs to be insulated from one department to other while they avail common database for generic details of the users/citizens.

Another important factor is the interaction between the database administrators of the state government and the different departments. Their daily functional interaction and data updating should see the smooth operations of the system. This requires a perfect reporting and structured query system.

Data maintenance

The true success is where the department is able to leverage the central data warehouse with its database to meet the additional needs of the users. To evolve an overall successful structure of the DBMS, it requires high flexibility to accommodate additional data load and keep equip to increase the processing speed and interaction with inter-departmental data warehouse. E-governance applications most often are the tools only to deliver to the citizens and it does not need decision support system as parameters to deliver. Therefore, it is simpler to optimize the system transactional load on the central system.

Considering the Indian scenario, it is ideal to design the architecture of the department first and the state government next, which requires extensive coordination at all levels of the government organizations. Perhaps, a detailed exercise to seek coordination can be the first step of the consultants' initiation towards e-governance.

Network security aspects

Computer security addresses the protection of information that is stored on a computer from unwanted access, while network security protects information that is being transmitted from unwanted access. Network security is required because of several reasons. Every year, numerous computer viruses attack networks throughout the world and disturb their normal operation. This shows that there are people who put in a lot of efforts to hack (or attack) information. Viruses are addressed by computer security measures but the main point is that information in transit can also be hacked by such people who will go to the extent of using or building software/hardware to do the job. Some of the ways in which hackers can access information in transit are given below:

- The main broadcast networks are Ethernet1, Wireless and CATV networks. Certain transmission links are broadcast by nature; in other words, multiple people can listen to what is being sent on these links.
- Even if the transmission link is point to point, the determined intruder can tap this link to access information.

So, if information sent between two users 'A' and 'B' has to remain confidential, it has to be encrypted. This security service is called confidentiality. But then how can user 'A' be sure that he is talking to user 'B' and no one else. There could be an intruder 'C' sitting in the middle, who is pretending that he is 'A' or 'B'. For example, 'C' could send messages to 'A' using the IP address of 'B' (called IP spoofing). So, it is necessary to be sure about the authenticity of the communicating peer. There is still a problem. 'C' sitting between 'A' and 'B' need not build any messages himself but can simply change the messages created by 'A' or 'B' or can alter the sequence of messages. In other words, it is not enough to ensure the authenticity of the peer; the integrity of the received message must also be verified. All this functionality is provided by the authentication security service.

In a government set-up of the data structure almost remain static. A small part may remain as dynamic data. Therefore, the network design need not be complex. However, data related to revenue sources and payment of subsidy to categories of social beneficiaries etc. deserve high security network design.

Other critical success factors

When implementing restructuring or changes in the administration, the management strategy must choose some basic characteristics that form part of change project. In the first place, the changes may be incremental or radical. Secondly, they must choose the tools for change and inducing factors or catalysts (rules, technology, professional roles, etc). One has to create a vision-shared that is realistic, market it and then develop a *modus operandi* realizing that vision. The primary requirement for integration is the systematic sequential order of modules as per the functional use. But, the integration depends on the combination of technical and organizational consensus as follows:

- Technical sophistication
- Organizational objectives
- Desirable changes in people's work conditions
- Design, develop and implement within the budget and time restrictions

A successful implementation includes certain aspects that are very critical though not new.

Managing the change

E-governance in reality is a process of implementing change management in the work culture, as it is understood through case studies in previous chapters. E-governance is not about computers and technology but it is more to do with the way one uses information and communications technology (ICT) as a mechanism for managing reforms. It has an effect on the relationship between government and citizens and between different government departments. Successful implementation and sustenance of e-governance requires planning, political will and a persistent dedication of resources. Mechanisms to motivate and change mindset can be brought in by various marketing techniques of ICT industry.

As the case studies reveal that a highly motivated champion can bring any e-governance projects in wide spectrum like education, tax reforms, urban governance and licence regulation etc. A common theme that can be understood from the case studies presented in this book is the change management, but the technology leverages vary from smart card applications to artificial intelligence technology. Where participation of common man is involved, a well-established project cannot be killed, despite the efforts put in by vested interests. If the project is user-friendly and adds value to the quality of life, citizens' pressure would generate force to use the system to its optimum. Operation and maintenance may cause inconveniences, but a citizen-centric project would always create demand for optimal use.

Stakeholder participation

One of the important objectives for success is to devise a mechanism for obtaining feedbacks from key stakeholders. This will help in 'strategic ownership' of the inevitable changes arising from the transition to e-governance reforms. The extent of participation relies on consultations between key stakeholders in government, business/private sector and civil society. Participation may occur in areas related to public services, in decision-making and in matters related to policy decisions.

Leadership

Most of the successful e-governance initiatives have been possible because of the champions who initiated and drove the project. In any dynamic organizational structure like government, departments may face problems if there is a break in linkages because of transfer of the initiator. The turnover of high and middle level managers in government departments often leaves the consultants and solution providers to start from scratch as and when there is a change of managers. It is impossible for any consultant to get into the shoe of every new manager arriving at the scene during the implementation period. When the vision and the strategic plans get mingled up leading to unforeseen situation, it is very difficult for any consultant to fill the gap. Hence, there is a need for governments to take a clear view to provide adequate time for development and implementation of such projects.

It is also important for the project initiator that in the present method of functioning, there is not much time to carry out studies, lengthy consultation process, report preparation to generate vision, strategic plan or for alternative solution development. One needs to grasp the problems quickly, arrive at the ultimate goal, and adopt rapid decision and implementation process. The project gestation has to be very short—may be 12 to 18 months!

Employees

While designing the system, it is important to understand that those who are presently operating the system can do their best in analyzing the existing system gaps and then suggest alternatives. Once system design is determined, employees' involvement should be planned at various stages of system integration. It is better to formulate a team of members having positive outlook, clean image and willingness to work. This employees' involvement from design stage will become a great source of success at the implementation stage too. It creates feeling of ownership of the project among the participants that enhances the chances of success in the project. This would also reduce training needs at subsequent level. Unless the leader of the e-governance project is a system integrator who possesses skills of insight judgement and creativity, it is difficult to achieve this socio-technical perspective.

Consultants/Solution providers

The role of the consultants or the total solution provider is vital in the successful implementation of e-governance projects. Normal government organizational structure does not have professional expertise in ICT and therefore there is a great compulsion to outsource technology-based expertise. When e-governance solutions are sought, neither the government managers nor the solution providers are aware about the likely solutions to be implemented. Hence, detailing out the components involved and estimated likely cost would be very difficult at the initial stage. When budget estimates for projects are prepared, almost one year in advance for the next financial year, estimate for civil infrastructures may be possible but it is impossible to estimate an e-governance project. This leads to a situation where the consultants have to prepare the project as per government budget.

It is easier to estimate hardware, software, networking and database management costs for a design which has been already prepared. When the scopes are not defined and definite solutions are still far from finalization, it is very difficult for any consultant to consider the project size and cost. This warrants a cohesive thinking between the government department seeking e-governance solutions and the consultants who would like to undertake such projects.

Outsourcing possibility

E-governance assignments are always multi-vendor assignments involving multiple systems and multiple technologies. The applications developer has to take care of integrating the main application with other systems and sub-systems. Outsourcing is the delegation of one or more IT-enabled processes to a third party that warns, administers and manages the business process according to a defined set of metrics. Part or full outsourcing depends on the flexibilities built in the project.

Public-private partnership is an integral part of e-governance outsourcing opportunities. This partnership would help in creating e-governance infrastructure, design, content and maintenance of portals, and integration and processing of transactions on a cost-sharing basis. Public-private partnership would also peg responsibility towards citizens while delivering face-to-face services through private agency at a minimum fee. This not only increases the relationship between government and citizens but also opens opportunities to receive suggestions and improve the services as desired by citizens.

Organizational responsibility

As governmental organizations have to undergo series of changes in terms of structure as well as processes, the successful adoption to changing needs would determine the level of benefits of the project. As the change from static paper processes to new structure, demand for addition of parallel processes arises. One need to be cautious in creating parallel processes or else the new system would become inefficient. Because of the change over, some redundancies in human and other resources become visible. Successfully redeploying these would be a critical task.

Top level commitment

Top-level commitment is, in fact, a factor that many analysts consider critical in administrative reforms, particularly in the field of e-governance. It has, however, different aspects. It involves not only the degree of commitment of senior management but also the ways in which this commitment is transmitted through the chain of command. Adequate budgetary resource allocation is also part of the responsibility of the top-level decisions.

Accountability and transparency

Accountability is something that differentiates a public organization from other types of organizations. Accountability also represents a preferred area for reflection in the field of e-governance, as we have seen. Equally, it is linked with the processes of building citizenship that occur, implicitly or explicitly, on configuring the procedures for the provision of services.

Transparency is related to the volume and quality of information provided to the public on the administration's activities. This information may refer to both services and specific processes, and in this case may contain both personal or aggregate information, and processes of decision-making or the mechanisms of implementing public policies. It also includes the availability of information on the rules and regulations related to a service and the commitments undertaken by the administration (response time, possibility of claims, consulting files, etc.).

Institutional and human resources strategy

Institutional and human resources ultimately determine the long-term sustainability of the project. The view the government adopts in these matters is critical. The most difficult task is of dealing with surplus staff, which, in some cases, would be large.

Governments with large pool of staff hired for life have always faced with problem of making its human resources IT savy. Several aspects of human resources management are critical. First of all, from among the pool of resources, which has practised a culture in which efficiency has little or no value, teams which work will have to be built up, motivated and made to participate in the systems development and implementation. From experience, it has been found that within the existing set-up a large number of capable people exist. Environment of trust is to be created with transparent administration. Further, they need to be adequately empowered and the process to be truly participatory. With such environment the chances of success of the project can be enhanced. Training and redeployment of some would be necessary. It is important to note that all activities have to be developed in-house and through employees' participation.

Legal framework

Automation of delivery systems and removal of manual procedures require a great understanding of existing laws, procedures, authentication and security etc. To meet these requirements, prior to the system design, a thorough understanding of all the aspects is required to build a framework for re-engineering processes of functions and activities.

Government officers are authorized to issue approvals or conduct government transactions after due verification of stipulated procedures. Hence, they are held responsible for any orders issued, which may not be duly verified and procedures not followed. Removal of such manual interventions requires legal authentication by changing the law to suit computerized verifications and authentications. On the other side, increasing cyber crime incidences makes security aspects of e-governance systems more vulnerable. Democratic governments may have to face more challenges while modifying the legal framework to suit the IT-based e-governance systems.

Most of the government data are confidential and deserve highest security. Any security breach through cyber crime is a major threat to the government. Hence, electronic signatures, electronic records and electronic authentications need to be foolproof. These have to be taken care through design of system architecture, programmes inscription, biometric authentication, mixing of part manual authentication, multi-level firewalls etc. However, these measures could not be adequate enough to certify for an outright change in the legal framework to suit e-governance systems. The case studies presented show the practical approach to comply with the existing legal framework instead of attempting to change the law.

Conclusion

Citizen-centric and revenue-generating projects related to licencing, tax regulations, urban governance or education have shown trends of achieving desired results. Though the case studies presented differ from each other in contents, stakeholders and customers, certain common themes emerge.

First of all, it is important to realize that a combination of strong motivation and sincere efforts can replace the cumbersome and lengthy procedures by best practices. Otherwise, the task of motivating stakeholders to replace old manual system with new e-governance system is difficult. There cannot be a uniform method to motivate the stakeholders to commit to these changes. Different strategies need to be planned and well-thought of actions have to be implemented, which would make the stakeholders commit to the change management and volunteer in the process.

The cases also reveal that a personal commitment of decision makers has an important impact on the intensity and shape of the end-results. In all of the case study projects, the success by and large is perceived through elimination of manual procedures, which consequently helped in achieving customers' satisfaction. While there is a scarcity of time in attending to the routine office works, finding time and space to think of innovation and creativity to change the existing delivery system requires great drive within oneself. The dream could not have materialized without strong self-motivation of the leaders.

Another important fact to consider is the political power structure. In an elected government, the system derives power from the elected body. Periodical changes in governments may lead to overnight changes in policy outlook making it difficult to implement e-governance systems. The same has been proved from the case studies that trust and commitment from the elected political bodies encourage the implementation of e-governance projects much faster.

All over the world, citizens think that their governments are very slow and poor in delivery systems. To commit and involve such stakeholders, the speed of implementation plays key role. Had the projects been completed as designed within time, it would have yielded even better results. Hence, at the design stage itself, one must plan to display the speed. This would prevent the negative and invisible forces that normally hamper implementation of any new project. A visible result, which removes the customers' inconvenience and provides more flexibilities and opportunities to get the things done, can be a major driving force of the customers to support innovations in e-governance systems.

While one is configuring the system, it is difficult to judge whether to go for a pilot project first or directly implement the comprehensive plan. However, the case studies have shown that the total replacement of the old system has proved better. It helps in compulsorily adopting the new system faster by the employees as well as the customers.

Overall, changes of this scale in the system are only possible with far-sighted visions of the leaders, skill to differentiate between technology and human resource management and commitment to work. With due consideration of the above, one can move forward to join hands with the future and create a good governance environment.

Annexures

Annexure I

Rates of motor vehicle tax as per Bombay Motor Vehicles Tax Act, 1958

Sr. No.	*Category of vehicles*	*Rate of tax (Rs)*
1	Motor-cycles	
	Not exceeding 50 kg. in weight unladen	500
	Exceeding 59 kg. but not exceeding 100 kg. in weight unladen (mopeds)	1,000
	Exceeding 100 kg. in weight, unladen (scooters, motor-cycles)	2,000
2	Three-wheelers (auto-rickshaws)	
	Part-I: Petrol-driven vehicles up to	
	3 passengers	2,500
	4 passengers	8,000
	5 passengers	8,900
	6 passengers	9,800
	Part-II: Diesel-driven vehicles	The rates shown in Part-I plus surcharge of 50%
3	Motor cars, private jeeps and private omni buses	
	Part-I: Petrol-driven vehicles	5% of the cost of vehicle (ex-factory price)
	Part-II: Diesel-driven vehicles	7.5% of the cost of vehicle
4	Taxi cab	
	Part-I: Petrol-driven vehicles	5% of the cost of vehicle
	Part-II: Diesel-driven vehicles	7.5% of the cost of vehicle
5	Light goods vehicles	
	Part-I: Petrol-driven vehicles	
	Vehicles registered, laden weight of which exceeds 750 kg.	4,400

Contd...

Sr. No.	Category of vehicles	Rate of tax (Rs)
	Vehicles registered, laden weight of which exceeds 750 kg. but does not exceed 1,500 kg	7,400
	Vehicles registered, laden weight of which exceeds 1,500 kg. but does not exceed 3,000 kg.	12,800
	Part-II: Diesel-driven vehicles	The rates shown in Part-I plus surcharge of 50%
6	Stage carriages (rates effective from 1.8.1990) Part-I: Petrol-driven vehicles	Annual rate of tax
	Passengers are more than 6 but less than 9	Rs. 600 plus Rs. 60 for every passenger in addition to six passengers.
	More than 9 passengers	Rs. 840 plus an amount calculated at the following rates in respect of passengers In excess of 9 namely: Rs. 72 per seating accommodation for every such passenger, and Rs. 36 per standing accommodation for every such passenger.
	Part-II: Diesel-driven vehicles	The rates shown in Part-I plus a surcharge of 50% subject to the maximum limit of Rs. 636.
7	Private service vehicles (rates effective from 1.4.2000) Part-I: Petrol-driven vehicles	Rs. 200 for every person permitted to be carried.
	Part-II: Diesel-driven vehicles	The rates shown in Part-I plus 50% surcharge subject to the maximum limit of Rs. 1,100.
8	Sleeper coaches (rates effective from 1.4.2002) Part-I: Petrol-driven vehicles	
	Sleeper designed omni buses licenced to carry not more than 20 passengers	Rs. 9,000 per passenger, which the vehicle is licenced to carry.
	Sleeper designed omni buses licenced to carry more than 20 passengers	Rs. 12,000 per passenger, which the vehicle is licenced to carry.

Contd...

Sr. No.	Category of vehicles	Rate of tax (Rs)	
9	Contract carriages (rates effective from 17.8.2001)		
	Ordinary designed omni buses		
	Up to 12 seats	Rs. 1,200 per seat	
	13 to 20 seats	Rs. 2,700 per seat	
	More than 20 seats	Rs. 3,600 per seat	
	Luxury/tourist designed omni buses		
	Up to 20 seats	Rs. 4,500 per seat	
	More than 20 seats	Rs. 6,000 per seat	
10	Goods vehicles (exceeding 3,000 kg. in weight, unladen) rates effective from 1.4.1997	Rate for petrol-driven vehicles (Rs.)	Rates for diesel-driven vehicles (Rs.)
	Up to 750 kg. gross vehicle weight	440	585
	Exceeding 750 kg. but not exceeding 1,500 kg.	740	1,010
	Exceeding 1,500 kg. but not exceeding 3,000 kg.	1,275	1,688
	Exceeding 3,000 kg. but not exceeding 4,500 kg.	1,640	2,235
	Exceeding 4,500 kg. but not exceeding 6,000 kg.	2,490	3,285
	Exceeding 6,000 kg. but not exceeding 7,500 kg.	3,070	3,930
	Exceeding 7,500 kg.	Rs. 3,070 plus Rs. 165 for every 250 kg. or part thereof in excess of 750 kg.	Rs. 3,070 plus a surcharge of 50% subject to the maximum limit of Rs. 1,800
11	Tractors (rates effective from 1.4.2003)	4% of the cost of diesel-driven vehicles	

For moffussil services 17.5 per cent of the inclusive amount of fares payable to the operator of stage carriages. For city services 1 per cent of the inclusive amount of fares payable to the operator of stage carriage.

Annexure II

Types of vehicles, their periodicity and dates from which the tax rate is effective

Sr. No.	*Type of vehicles*	*Periodicity*	*Date from which current rates are effective*
1	Two-wheelers	Lump sum (one time tax)	Up to 100 kg. in weight w.e.f. 3.4.1992 and exceeding 100 kg. in weight w.e.f. 1.8.1995.
2	Motor cars, private jeeps, private omni buses	Lump sum	1.8.1998
3	Auto-rickshaws, taxi cab	Lump sum	1.4.1999
4	Light goods vehicles (up to 300 kg. gross vehicle weight) such as chhakda delivery vans)	Lump sum	1.9.2001
5	Goods vehicles (exceeding 3,000 kg. gross vehicle weight)	Half yearly or annually	1.4.1997
6	Stage carriages	Quarterly or annually	1.8.1990
7	Contract-carriage buses	Monthly or annually	17.8.2001
8	Private service vehicles	Quarterly or annually	1.4.2000
9	Special purpose vehicles such as cranes, loaders, mortar graders, dumpers	Quarterly or annually	1.8.1995

Annexure III

E-governance: Operational Components

E-governance represents a new way of delivering services and there are two different facets of the system:

1. Operational part
2. Implementation part

For smooth functioning of the system, both of the above aspects have to be considered and the requirements of each one have to be met as per the context. Implementation part is discussed through various case studies in this annexure. This annexure specifically talks about the operational part of e-governance, including certain technology decisions. For a successful operation, the tasks of data management and networking have to be redefined as per the context and then implemented.

Elements of e-governance operation

Governance arrangements vary as per different types of public services as well as between the state sector and local government level. It is necessary to establish some kind of network among all of them. Another part arises from the need to provide opportunities for greater public participation in government, including a voice in the e-governance development process. Interaction with public is also a must for various functions related to civic service delivery like revenue collection etc.

There will be new challenges for the governance, as the general public and other private agencies become part of a more integrated style of government departments. The challenge is to ensure successful management of change and then maintain the same. It will demand for better transparency, responsibility, accountability, and prudent financial and operational management on government's part. Considering all these, e-governance needs decision-making processes that support more integrated data management system and strong networking.

In the early stages of e-governance, the major goal is to improve quality of service and people's overall experience with government through increased use of the Internet as an additional medium of interaction. Proper development of this new channel requires substantial investment across many agencies. It offers ways to achieve greater financial returns, but it will occur in the medium to long term and need to be actively managed.

The e-governance strategy's current response to increasing participation in democracy is to help people find government services and information using the portal. New technologies will enable easier access to government informations and processes. People will be well informed and better able to participate.

- Make government information easier to find.
- Publish key government information online.
- Provide multiple channels for contact with government.

There are some supporting activities connected with e-governance operation:

- Provide a secure environment and authentication framework enabling secured, trusted exchange of information among agencies and between agencies and customers.
- Catalogue government information.
- Drive the routine online publishing of key government information.
- Provide facilities to enable interactive consultation among agencies and between agencies and customers.
- Develop systems to enable the public to offer structured feedback on policy issues.

Data management

The quality of the data held by government agencies presents a major challenge for the e-governance programme. As they integrate different services and deliver them to people, more data will be exchanged or shared between different departments. This means that departments will have to plan to make ongoing investments in the quality of their data, both individually and in concert with other related departments. These costs will have to be incurred if the longer-run benefits of e-governance are to be realized and sustained. Therefore, while investing into new system, one has to decide upon the kind of technology to look for. An e-governance initiative is defined as a project or activity that involves the use of ICT to:

- interface to the public;
- support the delivery of services or information;
- automate 'back-office' systems, applications, and information resources that make up the agency's business; and
- align with strategic outcomes.

It can be fulfilled by certain back-office data management systems like ERP, e-GIF and shared workspace.

Enterprises resources planning

The shift to web enable government requires certain enabling technologies such as smart cards, digital signatures and certificates, electronic forms and so forth. To support these, a reliable transaction infrastructure has to be built. The need for cross-departmental communications, better access to applications and information led to the adoption of enterprise resources planning (ERP).

ERP systems are management information systems that integrate and automate many of the business practices associated with the operation or production aspects of a company. These typically include manufacturing, logistics, distribution, inventory, shipping, invoicing and accounting.

With help of ERP, order fulfilment tasks of a business process are automated. It involves taking an order from a customer, shipping it and billing for it. The process starts from the first stage of getting the work order where customer service representative takes all the necessary customer-related information. The advantage of ERP is that everyone else in other departments can also view this same information and have access to the database holding same order. So, when one department finishes with their job, it is automatically routed to the next department. Moreover, if one wants to find out the status of the order at any point, it takes only to log in to the system and check it. Thus, the whole thing moves in a swift way through different departments.

For the successful implementation of an ERP, the business organization and the technical solution provider firm have to negotiate about the requirements and adjustments possible. It is possible that the organization will need to change its way of doing business; at the same time, some need-based modifications in the standard ERP package available in the market may be necessary.* These things have to be discussed at the time of signing the contract between both the agencies so that chances of failure are minimized.

Another important part while implementing ERP is the cost component, as the price to be paid is heavy. Oversights in financial planning can send the costs of an ERP project spiralling out of control. While preparing the cost-benefit analysis, the financial executives must calculate the cost of software, consulting, process reworking, integration testing and other miscellaneous expenses against the benefits of ERP start appearing.

The critical areas of concern are:

- The price of teaching users their new job processes.
- Data warehouse integration requirements.
- The cost of extra software to duplicate the old report formats.
- Time spent after whole operation.

Once in place, ERP will provide the foundation for e-governance transactions that need to interact with financial and human resource systems such as online permits, licences and procurement. ERP is more to do with back-office system integration, in spite of the great pressure for applications that show quick visible results.

---

* In anticipation to this, the vendors have already started shifting from government's specific web enabled versions of their software to modules for tax management, public-private partnerships and so on.

E-governance interoperability framework

The e-governance system should have both inter- and intra-departmental data communication networks. For efficiency purpose, there will be a great need to develop and introduce a standardized system of decision-making processes about investment, development and management of IT resources across various governmental departments. These standard processes would enable different interrelated departments to work together to provide information and services to the public.

The e-governance interoperability framework (e-GIF) applies in instances of interoperability (i.e., shared information, technology and business processes) that provides good practice guidance for internal aspects of department information and technology management. e-GIF is a set of policies, technical standards and guidelines (recommended practices) covering data and information, ICT, and inter-agency electronic business protocols in the public sector. Working groups comprising government and vendors work on the production of this document.

As much as interoperability is about agencies working together to improve delivery of services, it also impacts the vendor community, in that they need to understand and provide services based on inter-agency business needs. Contribution by the vendor community in the formative stages of e-GIF is an important factor to ensuring the validity of the framework. A document such as the e-GIF must change as technology and business needs change, otherwise it is meaningless. This will be assured through design of appropriate governance arrangements for the e-GIF, which will guide future change to the policies, standards and guidelines in a way that should be both measured and responsive.

The e-GIF need to be kept under constant development so that it remains fit for purpose. Any private or public organization can form a working group, which can address either a gap in the framework or updating the existing components.

The e-GIF shall:

- Provide government departments an underlying platform of fixed, known and common elements that helps in the process of making sound decisions about investment, development and management of IT resources.
- Allow government departments to communicate faster.
- Allow employees within government departments to concentrate on maximizing the use of their resources to provide the customers with better services.
- Not compromise people's rights to privacy and security of their personal information held with government departments in any way.

Shared workspace

Shared workspace is an initiative that can form part of back-office systems (when used for collaboration) and also deliver information (when used as an Intranet).

Purpose of shared workspace

The main goal of shared workspace is to facilitate government employees with secure sharing of information within team members or across organizational boundaries and set good practice. The purposes of the shared workspace are:

- Implement a shared set of tools and services for secured online collaboration, for diverse teams/communities in government and their business partners.
- Facilitate better understanding and use of online collaboration for those working across agency boundaries.
- Help agencies to share their highest value documents and data.

Shared workspace is an optional 'input' to agency networking processes, so it is essential that it should always focus on meeting agency and user needs. For successful implementation of shared workspace, there are some requirements that should be met with:

- Secure sharing
- Familiar tools
- Matching type of groups and online tools
- Clear business drivers
- Standard methods of use for the workspace

Infrastructure and applications: The shared workspace offers a modular, online, 'toolbox' of applications. Criteria for selection of infrastructure are:

- Suited to the intended use
- Based on standards
- Value for money
- Fits with existing hosting environment.

Criteria for selection of applications software are:

- Generic
- Known to be needed by cross agency group
- Already familiar to users, where possible
- Available from a range of suppliers
- Available for reasonable cost.

Tool selection is user-needs driven. For each tool, there is a prototyping or mock-up stage so that they can then make concrete suggestions and test with real data. This puts the valuable user input upfront—at the earlier stage where changes can be easily made freeing up resources for other work. Suppliers should be also made aware of the fact of implementing only the successful prototypes. The shared workspace can be undertaken in three phases as under:

- *Phase 1—Investigation:* This phase should include exploration of past work on the secured exchange of information, literature search to discover current thinking and practice in terms of policy development, assessment of the use of electronic applications in other jurisdictions, and development of a high level concept of an electronic shared workspace.

- *Phase 2—Focus group discussions*: This phase should include interviews and a series of focus group discussions with a range of policy managers and analysts, and other stakeholders; and also surfacing of potential opportunities and issues and examination of benefits and risks.
- *Phase 3—Clarify the concept of shared workspace*: This phase should include establishing potential functionality and operational requirements, identify potential benefits to the public service, identify possible barriers to successful implementation, and specify the organization and management requirements to operate a shared workspace application across the public service.

Security principles

For confidential reasons, it is necessary to apply some safety controls on shared data under the system. Therefore, most shared workspace systems are accredited and certified for 'in confidence'. Shared workspace programme will be getting resources and keeping accreditation and certification. As part of this process, the shared workspace programme will have an independent party audit that configuration and handling of hardware, software, data, back-ups and traffic are to government-endorsed security standards. This audit will be repeated annually. Users of the tools are responsible for making sure that they are not sharing data that is classified higher than the shared workspace tool is accredited for.

A shared workspace will make it easier to work across government departments by:

- using existing technical infrastructure (computers, cables, servers, e-mail);
- improving management of multi-department networks, committees, teams and projects;
- making better use of the business information from a range of sources;
- providing a simpler way of distributing and gathering information; and

- not replacing face-to-face meetings between public servants.

Geo-spatial Information

Geo-spatial information is the convenient way of managing spatial or location-related information across government departments. With help of this, information like addresses, road and place names etc. can be shared over the Internet. Geo-spatial information is vital for a wide range of government functions. For example, it is necessary for running an election, registering people against the correct electoral voters' list, or helping to achieve emergency services' responses, the management of civil defence emergencies, or underpinning land use decisions. The government should make sure that addresses road and place names information used nationally is fit for these purposes, consistent, up-to-date, and readily accessible.

Geo-spatial information should be rationalized and managed to:

- achieve consistent ways of describing place information across all state governments and their departments; and
- allow people to easily search through government portal for location-related information.

Procurement process

Computerized procurement process provides ways for government departments to collaborate in buying goods and services through syndicated procurement, adoption of best practice processes and e-procurement initiatives. This would improve the purchase of goods and services. This includes the processes, culture and information technology necessary to attain leading procurement practices. The procurement process comprises three interrelated initiatives:

- Syndicated procurement
- Best practice processes
- E-procurement

Syndicated procurement

Syndicated procurement is where government departments collectively procure goods and services through multi-agency agreements or contracts. This will result in savings from lower prices, improved terms and conditions, improved service levels and reduced tendering costs.

Syndicated procurement builds on the 'strategic sourcing' approach being taken by leading government departments. Strategic sourcing refers to the disciplined process by which an organization defines and segments its requirements for all goods and services, understands the supply market, and negotiates with suppliers accordingly.

Best practice processes

The best practice processes initiative is exploring ways that agencies can more efficiently organize 'back-office' procurement operations including requisitioning, tender, fulfilment, payment, and accounting processes. This is being done through departments' sharing knowledge and expertise so that all government departments can potentially lift their performance.

E-procurement

E-procurement is the use of e-commerce technology and processes for procurement activities. Information technology is required to sustain savings from syndicated procurement and best practice processes. In particular, the following aspects of e-procurement will be used:

- Electronic requisitioning and approvals
- Electronic catalogues
- Data collection and reporting of procurement information
- Interfacing into agency and supplier back-end systems (e.g., financial management systems)

E-commerce

While the e-governance programme is concerned with delivering services online, there should be a consideration that smaller companies and companies in the regions get the opportunity to develop their online capability. The e-commerce programme could ensure businesses and see to it that the country's infrastructure supports the needs of the knowledge economy.

E-services

The vision for e-governance should be the one, which is able to find public information and services within government departments quickly and easily over the Internet. Therefore, the e-services project should:

- identify which government services can be offered online when the portal goes live;
- identify common services between government departments to avoid double-ups; and
- ensure their individual expertise in offering services online is used.

E-billing and e-payments

A strategy for electronic billing and payment systems enables government agencies to carry out financial transactions securely over the Internet, either between each other or with people.

Electronic billing and payments should:

- enable people to receive bills and make payments to government over the Internet within an agreed policy framework and to agreed standards; and
- lead to the development of a common secure online transactional facility across government agencies.

Online authentication

An all-of-government framework (and potentially a 'solution') for online authentication has to be developed to ensure that government services delivered over the Internet are going to the right person and their privacy is protected. This can be achieved by electronically verifying that people are who they say they are, and that privacy is protected at all times.

E-governance network

At the state government level, there should be e-governance steering committee to oversee the implementation and determine requirements for future sustenance. The responsibilities of the committee include:

- acting as a conduit for two-way communication between their organization and the e-governance unit;
- ensuring mandatory requirements from the programme are included into their organization's work plan; and
- working within their organization to ensure that the approach to online service delivery is consistent with the policies and standards developed in the e-governance programme.

Two CIO (Chief Information Officer) networks support the managers who are accountable for the design and delivery of the technical and information management dimensions of e-governance. The CIO networks (one for policy departments and another for operational departments) typically focus on the implementation of the interoperability framework, keep a check on technical standards and guidelines and controls government IT infrastructure. The important tasks are described below:

Assessment and monitoring

- Keep track of individual government department projects that contribute to the facilitation of electronic government.
- Develop an online means for government departments to share information about their e-governance activities.

Measuring the uptake and effectiveness of e-governance

It is important to measure progress towards achieving the mission regularly and consistently. The e-governance network should have a research and evaluation framework to monitor the success of the programmes.

Measuring uptake of e-governance by agencies (input focus)

- Adoption of policies, standards and solutions developed for common use. The extent to which business plans or other accountability documents incorporate e-governance.
- The extent to which agencies deliver their identified e-governance results, particularly those that relate to the all-of-government priorities for online service delivery.
- Publication of all-of-government e-governance uptake results by the e-governance unit.
- The above processes can be reviewed with the e-governance unit and State Services Commission Team where appropriate.

Measuring the effectiveness of e-governance (output focus)

- Measurement framework for customer satisfaction with online services, including accessibility and uptake by people and businesses (agencies would be responsible for measuring this with customers using online and offline services).
- Initial substantial costs of e-governance are balanced in the longer term by savings in agencies (agencies would be responsible, with e-governance unit support, for identifying the fiscal and economic benefits of their e-governance application portfolios over time).
- Government internal process improvement to support higher volumes and better quality through core work by staff (joint responsibility of the e-governance unit and agencies to determine the cost and benefits prior to and after changes).

By measuring a series of inputs and outputs, the research and evaluation framework will enable the tracking of uptake and effectiveness of e-governance in several ways. This can help in providing a way to pick up early warnings and identify real progress.

Portal

A portal is a single website giving structured access to other websites of all the government departments. It is a convenient way of finding out about government informations and services from one place, without having to understand how government is structured and therefore which sites you need to use.

Portals are usually grouped by industry or sector type, for example, health, education, building industry. They are sometimes organized as per types of services, for example, registration and licencing, or purchasing. The portal shall be a website providing search capability for, and links into the online and off-line information and services of most government agencies.

It is easy to find information with help of a portal. Government is currently describing online and off-line information and services using a consistent classification system. The result is an integrated catalogue of information that you can search through the Internet.

So, if one searches on 'licence', he/she would be given a choice of, for example, marriage/dog/gun/driver licences. Often, the way government describes something and what a person call it are two different names—a good example is what one calls a dog licence, a local body may call a canine registration. The government shall make sure that if one is looking for a particular government service or piece of public information, and then one should find it.

Therefore, a government portal should provide a single Internet address through which you can search for online and off-line government information and services without having to go to individual government agency websites and also provide a complementary alternative to across the counter and telephone contact with government.

Bibliography

Books

Andreasen, A.R., (1995), Marketing Social Change: Changing Behaviour to Promote Health, Social Development and the Environment, San Francisco: Jossey-Bass Publications.

Ed. Chissick Michael and Harrington Justin, (2003), E-Government: A Practical Guide to the Legal Issues, Sweet & Maxwell.

Halfani, M., McCarney, P. and Rodriguez, A., (1998), Towards an Understanding of Governance: The Emergence of an Idea and Its Implications for Urban Research in Developing Countries, University of Toronto Press, Toronto, ON, Canada.

Mehta, Dinesh, (1998), Urban Governance: Lessons from Best Practices in Asia, UMP-Asia Occasional Paper No. 40.

Riley, Thomas B., (2003), International Tracking Survey Report '03- No. 04, E-government vs E-governance: Examining the Differences in a Changing Public Sector Climate.

SJB Research, Longport, UK, (April 1999), Biometric Technology Today, Volume 7, No. 1.

Van Der Meer, A. and Van Winden W., (2003), Regional Studies, Vol. 37.4, E-governance in Cities: A Comparison of Urban Information and Communication Technology Policies.

Websites

http://economictimes.indiatimes.com/ (January, 2004)

http://www.gdrc.org/u-gov/governance-define.html

http:/www.sjbresearch.com

Glossary

ANSI	American National Standards Institute
Application Software	To meet the specific functional and business requirements of the enterprise application software is used. It is the software form of the business logic, business rules and business requirements of the enterprise. Application Software typically forms a layer on top of the System Software and the Database Software layers.
Application layer	Layer 7 of the OSI model. This layer determines the interface of the system with the user.
Application metadata	Data dictionary; data concerning the structure and contents of application menus, forms, and reports.
Application Programme	A custom-developed programme for processing a database. It can be written in a standard procedural language such as COBOL, C++,C or Visual Basic, or in a language unique to the DBMS.
Application Programme Interface (API)	A set of programme procedures or functions that can be called to invoke a set of services. The API includes the names of the procedures and functions and a description of the name, purpose, and data type of parameters to be provided. For example, a DBMS product could provide a library of functions to call for

	database services. The names of procedures and their parameters constitute the API for that library.
ASP	Active Serve Page. A file containing markup language; server script, and client script that is processed by the Active Server Processor in Microsoft IIS.
Asynchronous transfer mode	A form of packet transmission using fixed size packets, called ATM is the data transfer interface for B-ISDN. Unlike X.25, ATM does not provide error control and flow control mechanism.
Authentication*	A process used to verify the integrity of transmitted data, especially a message.
Backend	The computer systems that form the foundation of any IT project. Backend systems are not visible to the end users though they come into play each time a user interacts with the system. Only partial views of the data, information and business logic as needed contextually, are visible to the end user at the front-end in an appropriate user-friendly format. Database systems, security systems, operating systems, backup systems and so on form the backend.
Bandwidth*	The difference between the liming (upper and lower) frequencies of a continuous frequency spectrum.
BPR	Business Process Re-engineering. It is method by which age-old procedures existing in an enterprise are critically examined and revamped so as to align the functioning of the enterprise along the current needs of the customers.
Broadband	In general, wide bandwidth equipment or systems that can carry signals occupying a large portion of the electromagnetic spectrum. Typically, a broadband communication system can simultaneously accommodate voice, data, video, and other services. In digital transmission systems, the term connotes high data rate.

Build in function.	In SQL, any of the functions COUNT, SUM, AVG, MAX, or MIN.
Byte	A group of bits, usually eight, used to represent a character of other data.
Client computer	(1) A personal computer on a local area network with client-server architecture. In a database application, the client computer processes database application programmes. Requests for actions on the database are sent to the database computer. (2) In the three-tier and multi-tier architecture, a computer that hosts a browser for accessing a Web server.
Client-server database architecture	The structure of a networked computing system in which one computer (usually a personal computer) performs services on behalf of other computer, which is called a database server, processes the DBMS, and client computers process the application programmes. All database activities are carried out by the database server.
Client-server system	A system of two or more computers in which at least one computer provides services for one or more other computers. The services can be database services, communication services, printer services, or some other function.
CPU	Central Processing Unit; the portion of the computer hardware that processes arithmetic and logic instructions. The term CPU usually includes main memory as well.
DAFS	Direct Access File System. A high speed and reliable memory to memory transaction mechanism for accessing data from application servers.
Data mart	A facility similar to a data warehouse but for a restricted domain. Often the data are restricted to particular types, business functions, or business units.

Data administration	The function that concerns the effective use and control of the organization's data assets. It can be a person but more often is a group. Specific functions include setting data standards and policies and providing a forum for conflict resolution. Also see database administrator.
Data integrity	The state of a database in which all constraints are fulfilled; usually refers to inter-relation constrains in which the value of a foreign key is required to be present in the table having that foreign key as its primary key.
Data model	(1) A model of the users' data requirements expressed in terms of either the entity-relationship model or the semantic-object model. It is sometimes called a users' data model. (2) A language for describing the structure and processing a database.
Data Multipulation Language (DML)	A language used to describe the processing of a database.
Data source	In the ODBC standard, a database together with its associated DBMS, operating system, and network platform.
Data warehouse	A store of enterprise data that is designed to facilitate management decision making. A data warehouse includes not only data, but also metadata, tools, procedures, training, personnel, and other resources that make access to the data easier.
Database administration	The function that concerns the effective use and control of a particular database and its related applications.
Database Architecture	Data Architecture defines the way different components of an enterprise database are organized and positioned logically and physically. It is scenario where the data is generated in different locations in

	an enterprise; the database architecture becomes critical to performance.
Database server	(1) On a local area network with client-server database architecture, the computer that runs the DBMS and processes actions against the database on behalf of its client computers. (2) In the three-tier and multi-tier architecture, a computer that hosts a DBMS and responds to database requests from the Web server.
Database	A self-describing collection of integrated records.
Data-item	(1) A logical group of bytes in a record, usually used with file processing. (2) In the context of the relational model, a synonym for attribute.
DBMS engine	A DBMS subsystem that processes logical I/O requests from other DBMS subsystems and submits physical I/O requests to the operating system.
DBMS	Database Management System; a set of programmes used to define, Administrator, and process the database and its applications.
Distributed Database Management System (DDBMS)	In a distributed database, the collection of distributed transaction and database managers on all computers.
Distributed Database	A database stored on two or more computers. Distributed data can be partitioned or not partitioned, replicated or not replicated.
EIS	Enterprise Information System. An advancement of the concepts of MIS. EIS provides transaction level information of the various aspects of functioning of an enterprise. Usually, the information is available at a high level of abstraction, which can be drilled down to the required level of granularity and detail as needed.

e-Procurement	Electronic Procurement. It is an ICT system that enables efficient and transparent management of the process of procuring products, works and services on an end-to-end basis. e-Procurement can handle all the phases of procurement. e-Procurement reduces the cost of doing business and setting up a healthy competition between suppliers.
ERP	Enterprise Resource Planning. ERP is a resource management technology that integrates the enterprise-wide resources of a company. These operations include human resources, financial operations, manufacturing, and distribution. ERP also connects an organization to its customers and suppliers.
File data source	An ODBC data source stored in a file that can be E-mailed or otherwise distributed among users.
File server	In a local area network, a personal computer containing a file that it processes on behalf of other personal computers on the network. The term file server is normally used for the resource-sharing architecture. See Client computer, Client-server database architecture, Database server, and Resource-sharing architecture.
FTP	File Transfer Protocol. FTP is a TCP-based protocol that ensures the error-free transmission and downloading of programme and data files across remote networks and the Internet.
Gateway	Gateway, in relation to e-government is a core infrastructure that liberates the front-end access of the users from the backend implementations of the government agencies. A gateway performs certain common functions such as registration and authentication of the users, routine their requests for services to the appropriate backend and providing security services. The concept of gateway is innovative.
HTML	Hyper-Text Markup Language. HTML is the language used to design web-pages in a standards based

	manner such that it is possible to display the content of such pages using standard web browsers.
HTTP	Hypertext Transfer Protocol. The standard protocol that supports data transfers over the Web (WWW). Each HTTP based transaction consists of an ASCII request from the client-side browser and a server-side browser and a server-side response.
Hypertext Markup Language	A standardized system of tagging text for formatting, locating images and other non-text files, and placing links or reference to other documents.
ICT	Information and Communication Technologies. ICTs encompass a wide range of various types e.g. terrestrial, wireless and satellite, audio, video and data communications including all kinds of electronic media.
Internet	A world-wide, public network of computes that communicate using TCP/IP.
Inter-operatibility	Interoperatibility is the capability of disparate computer/information systems to 'talk' to each other or behave in such as manner as if they were parts of the same system. Interoperatibility of systems arises out of the open standards followed by all the systems in question.
Intranet	(1) A private local or wide area network that uses TCP/IP, HTML, and related browser technology on client computers and Web server technology on servers. (2) Less commonly, any private LAN or WAN that involves clients and servers.
ISDN	Integrated Services Digital Network: Technology that provides high speed (156 mbps) end-to-end digital connectivity by using digital telephone systems. ISDN can easily support bandwidth-intensive services, such as video on demand, live television, full-motion multimedia, and high-quality audio signals, in addition to text-based data signals.

LAN	Local Area Network; a group of microcomputers connected to one another by means of communication lines in close proximity, usually less than a mile.
Mbps	Mega Byte Per Second.
Metadata	Data concerning the structure of data in a database stored in the data dictionary. Metadata are used to describe tables, columns, constrains, indexes, and so forth. Computer this with Application metadata.
MIS	Management Information System. Also known as Business Intelligence (BI), MIS is the process of gathering, managing, and analyzing data on which future business decisions and operational processes are based.
Modem	Modulator-demodulator: Converts analog signals received from a telephone line into digital signals that a computer can process and vice versa.
Network data model	A data model supporting at least simple network relationship. The CODASYL, DBTG, which supports simple network relationships but not complex relationships, is the most important network data model.
Network	(1) A group of interconnected computers. (2) An intranet (3) The Internet.
Open Database Connectivity Standard (ODBC)	A standard interface by which application programmes can access and process SQL databases (or table structures such as spreadsheets and text tables) in a DBMS-independent manner. The driver manager portion of ODBC is incorporated into Windows; ODBS drivers are supplied by DBMS vendors, Microsoft, and by other third-party software developers.
OSS	Open Source Software. OSS is software, whose source code is made available to the users for examination, analysis and modification to suit one's needs.

	It is pitted against the proprietary software, whose code is held as an intellectual property (IP) by the manufacturer. Linux is the most popular of the OSS and is growing in market share.
PL/SQL	Programming language/SQL. An Oracle-supplied language that augments SQL with programming language structures such as while loops, if-then-else blocks, and other such constructs. PL/SQL is used to create stored procedures and triggers.
Portal	A portal is a gateway to several related web sites and applications on the Internet.
Protocol	A set of standards to facilitate communication between two network devices.
Proxy Server	Proxy Server is a server that masks the IP address of a computer within a network and assigns its own IP to data packets sent outside the system. This mechanism insulates the individual systems within a network from a direct exposure to the outside world and thus reduce the vulnerability to attacks.
RAID	Redundant Array of Inexpensive Disks. RAID is the method of distributing data across several storage disks. Five levels of RAID help in the efficient usage of the available bandwidth. The RAID levels also provide efficient methods of data recovery in the case of server crashes.
RDBMS	Relational Database Management System, RDBMS is a standards based system of storing data in a systematic manner, in a number of tables. The data in different tables can be retrieved and/or manipulated simultaneously preserving the inter-relationships of the data stored in the different tables. Use of RDBMS ensures the integrity and concurrency of all data records that are logically related to one another.
Relational data model	A data model in which data is stored in relations and relationships between rows are represented by data values.

Relational database	A database consisting of relations. In practice, relational database contain relations with duplicate rows. Most DBMS products include a feature that removes duplicate rows then necessary and appropriate. Such a removal is not done as a matter of course because it can be time-consuming and expensive.
Router	An internetworking device that connects two computer networks. It makes use of an internet protocol and assumes that all of the attaché devices on the networks use the same communications architecture and protocols. A router operates at OSI layer 3.
SAN	The latest storage solution technology that was developed to deal with large amounts of data securely and reliably without hampering overall network performance.
Schema	A compete logical view of the database.
Single Point of Failure	It is the weakest link or component in a large IT system that may cause disruption of the entire system by its failure since there is no redundancy provided for that component. The reliability and availability of IT systems increases to extremely high levels if all the Single Points of Failure are identified at the design stage and adequate redundancies and failover mechanisms are provided.
Smart Card	Smart Card is basically an electronic identity card that has a chip embedded in it. It carries a lot of data relating to the individual, for example, employee data, medical data, insurance data, driving licence.
SQL	Structured Query Language; a language for defining the structure and processing of a relational database. It is used as a stand-alone query language, or it may be embedded in application programmes. SQL is accepted as a national standard by the American National Standards Institute. It was developed by IBM.

SWAN	Storage wide-area network. A SAN that extends over a broad geographic area (hundreds and thousands of kilometres).
System Software	System Software is the bundle of software components that form the operating system, the security systems and the support systems that enable optimal utilization of all the computer resources in an enterprise system. The application software, which is the software equivalent of the business requirements of an enterprise, 'sits' on the system software.
TCP/IP	Transmission Control Protocol/Internet Protocol. It is the universal standard of transmitting data over the Internet through digital data packets having standard structure and construction. TCP/IP standard has made communication over the Internet incredibly efficient.
TRANSACT/SQL	A Microsoft-supplied language that is part of SQL Server. It augments SQL with programming language structures such as while loops, if-then-else blocks, and other such constructs. TRANSACT/SQL is used to create stored procedures and triggers.
Virus	Virus is malicious software developed and propagated by miscreants so as to adversely affect the data, applications and the operations of the users of systems infected by such virus.
WAN	Wide Area Network. It is a network that spans over large geographical areas.
Web server	In the three-tier architecture, a computer that sits between the client computers and the database depends on the existence of another entity.
Web Services Architecture	It is the emerging application architecture most suited to develop Internet-based applications for enterprises. It provides the standards and protocols for defining, publishing and discovering application services on the Internet. It is based on the principles

	of interoperability and reuse of applications in the web world.
WML (Wireless Markup Language)	It defines hypertext-like content and hypertext—like content and applications for handheld devices with small displays. It is designed to create web pages that remain easy to use and legible despite the limitations of these devices, which include small screen size, limited gray-scale or colour palette, limited input capabilities and narrow band network connectivity
WTLS (wireless transport layer security)	Wireless transport layer security is an optional security layer which has encryption facilities that provide the secure transport service required by a number of applications such as e-commerce.
WAP (Wireless Application Protocol)	Wireless Application Protocol has been designed to enable standard off-the-shelf internet servers to provide services to wireless devices. WAP in the future will include end-to-end security, smart card interfaces, connection oriented transport protocols, billing interfaces and evolution to support multi-media mobile services.
XML	Extended Markup Language. It is a standards-based computer language which itself-descriptive and is extensible or flexible to be defined in a manner that meets the exact requirements of the users.

Index

Ahmedabad city, 131-32
  city civic centres in, 145-46
Ahmedabad Municipal Corporation (AMC), 131-36, 161, 176
  e-governance in 141-57: need for, 140-41; benefits of, 157-58;
  governing structure of, 133-36
Andreasen, A.R., 32

Central Motor Vehicles Rules, 1989, 36-37
change management
  concept of, 31-33, 175
  in government departments, 183-90
  key challenges for, 176-77
  process of implementation, 177-83
city civic centres
  in Ahmedabad, 145-46,
    services offered at, 149
Commercial Vehicle, 96

driving licence
  need for, 36-39

e-governance, 26-27
  as a tool of change management, 34
  challenges for, 28-31: tactical, 29; strategic, 29-30
  objectives of, 27-28, 193
  process of, 21
e-government
  vs e-governance, 26
e-learning
  in Ahmedabad schools, 101-74

good governance
  criteria for, 23-24
governance, 21, 23-24
  dimensions of, 23
  government vs, 22-24
government programmes
  characteristics of, 25
government, 21-22
  characteristics of, 22
  vs governance, 22-24
Gujarat, 64

ICT (information and communication technology), 21, 24
  in government sector, application of, 24-25
IMIS (integrated management information system)
  benefits of, 114, 126
  in Gujarat transport department, 114-30
inter-state border transport check-posts
  activities undertaken by, 65
  automation of, 69-94: features of, 80, 82-87; hurdles faced in the, 87-89; benefits of, 92-94
  clearance procedure of, 86
  functioning of, 77
  in Gujarat, 63-65, 70
  key components of, 77
  problems in carrying out activities at, 65-68

Kettl, Donald F., 22

MIS, 114
Motor Vehicles Act, 1988, 36, 64, 95-96
municipal schools
  society's perception of, 163

optical card registration certificate book
  in Gujarat, 95-96

paper driving licence, 39
  and smart card licence, differences between, 54
  disadvantages of, 40-41
paper RC book
  problems of, 96-97
project implementation
  problems of, 194-205
  success factors in, 205-12

RC book
  purposes of, 96
road accidents
  in Gujarat, 37-38

schoolnet project, 162
  in Ahmedabad schools, 164-74: problems in, 172-73; results of, 174
smart card
  system functions of a, 43-46
smart card technology, 43
  constraints of, 59-60
smart card-based driving licence, 35-36
  and paper licence, comparisons between, 59
  benefits of, 53-59
  genesis of, 41-43
  in Gujarat, 35, need for, 36
  user-friendly features of, 56-58
smart optical RC book, 101
  benefits of, 106-10
  features of, 99, 101
SWOT analysis, 190-92

teachers' training
  in Gujarat, 166-69
training of trainers, 170-72

vehicle population
  in Gujarat, growth of, 97